GET HOUSE SMART

GET HOUSE SMART

Series Editor
Barbara Loos Chintz

Series Art Director
Barbara Rietschel

Associate Art Director
Andrew Ploski

Editor
Cinda Siler

Writers
Mark Feirer
Laura Tringali
Albert E. Sakavich
Pat Willard

Research Editors
Alex Brackman
Yvette Brackman

Picture Research Editors
Marion Bodine
Monique Boniol

Copy Editor
Gina Grant

Consultants
Larry Aguzzi
Mark Feirer
Libby Hutcheson
 of Houlihan/Lawrence
Bart Tyler
 of Kelloggs & Lawrence

Illustrators
John Hovell
Bob Steimle

Art Production
Robert Graf

Production Supervisor
Peg Hoh

Library of Congress Cataloging in Publication Data
Get house smart: the easy quick-start guide to the
workings of your home
          p.   cm. — (Reader's Digest Smart Series)
          Includes index.
ISBN 0–89577-981-1
1. Buildings—Mechanical equipment—Amateurs' manuals. 2. Dwellings—Amateurs' manuals. 3. Housekeeping.
I. Reader's Digest Association. II. Series.
TH6010.G4   1997
643—dc21   97-17441

The credits and acknowledgments that appear on pages 168 are hereby made a part of this copyright page.

GET

READER'S DIGEST SMART SERIES™

HOUSE
SMART

THE EASY QUICK-START
GUIDE TO THE WORKINGS
OF YOUR HOME

The Reader's Digest Association, Inc., Pleasantville, New York•Montreal

INTRODUCTION

Smart Guide:
The anatomy of a room, with its pertinent parts numbered and labeled.

Checklist: Points to consider before buying.

Shortcuts: Ways to save time and/or money.

Trouble: Tips about identifying problems and finding easy solutions.

When it comes to your house, ignorance is not bliss—it's expensive, annoying, and time-consuming. That's where GET HOUSE SMART comes in; it's your guide to the mystifying world of home owning. So before you buy, before you hire, before you sign, before you remodel, get the inside track on how your house works—and what to do when some part of it doesn't. Use the graphic tools below to see at a glance just what you need to know.

TIME FACTOR

READ

This page	1 min
Most pages	4 mins
One chapter	15-30 mins
Entire book	3-4 hrs

NOTE: Time Factor estimates do not include making a sandwich to eat while reading.

Time Factor: Estimates for how long a repair job should take and which professional should do it.

Note: Time Factor does not include time for setup and cleanup.

HOME CENTER RESOURCES

Ace Hardware	630-990-6600
Builders Square	800-634-5949
84 LUMBER	800-359-8484
Hechinger/Home Quarters	301-341-1000
HomeBase	800-481-2273
Home Depot	800-553-3199
Lowe's Companies	800-445-6937
Menard's	715-876-5911
Payless Cashways	816-234-6000
Sears	800-469-4663
Tru-Serve	412-283-4567

Resources: Phone numbers of key manufacturers and companies that can help you find what you need.

Feel free to contact us with your thoughts and comments at our Web site:
www.readersdigest.com

TABLE OF CONTENTS

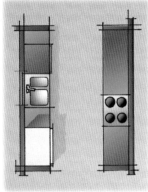

BUYING/SELLING

O n the stress scale, buying or selling a house is right up there with having root canal. Don't panic. Read on and get the inside story on buying and selling.

TIME FACTOR	
Inspection	4 hrs
Title search	2 wks
Mortgage	4-8 wks
Closing	2-8 hrs

SPEC SHEET

The specification or "spec" sheet lists the house's vital statistics. The data is entered and listed by licensed listing agents. The list itself is usually stored in the database of a local Multiple Listing Service (MLS). Note: The data and abbreviations will vary across the country.

LOCATION

1 . . . LISTING NUMBER

2 . . . AREA (as divided by MLS)

3 . . . TYPE OF PROPERTY (single family, condo, etc.)

4 . . . STATUS (active or in contract)

5 . . . LISTING PRICE

6 . . . ADDRESS

7 . . . POST OFFICE

8 . . . MUNICIPALITY

9 . . . NUMBER OF ROOMS

10 . . . ESTIMATED SQUARE FEET

11 . . . SCHOOL DISTRICT

12 . . . NUMBER OF BEDROOMS

13 . . . NUMBER OF BATHS

14 . . . NUMBER OF LEVELS

15 . . . DIMENSIONS OF LIVING ROOM

16 . . . DIMENSIONS OF MASTER BEDROOM

17 . . . NAMES OF SCHOOLS (elementary, junior & senior)

DESCRIPTION

18 . . . STYLE OF HOUSE (colonial)

19 . . . COLOR OF HOUSE

20 . . . ATTACHED/DETACHED

21 . . . MODEL (number or name of house in a development)

22 . . . LOT FRONTAGE (in feet)

23 . . . LOT DEPTH (in feet)

24 . . . EXTERIOR (clapboard)

25 . . . ACREAGE

26 . . . SHAPE OF PLOT (Regular [R] or Irregular [I])

27 . . . YEAR BUILT

28 . . . HOME OWNER'S ASSOC. (Yes or No)

29 . . . NEIGHBORHOOD ASSOC.

30 . . . ADDITIONAL FEE

TAXES

31 . . . TAX ID NUMBER

32 . . . ESTIMATED ANNUAL TAXES

33 . . . TAX YEAR

34 . . . PARTIAL ASSESSMENT

LEVELS

35 . . . LEVEL ONE (entry hall, living room, dining room, eat-in-kitchen, powder room, family room with door to deck)

36 . . . LEVEL TWO (master bedroom with whole bath, family bedrooms, hall bath)

37 . . . LEVEL THREE: (study)

38 . . . BASEMENT (finished)

39 . . . ATTIC

40 . . . POSSESSION (as soon as possible)

41 . . . ZONING (legal size of zoning parcels in that area: .5 acres)

PARTICULARS

42 . . . ITEMS INCLUDED IN SALE

43 . . . EXCLUDED ITEMS

44 . . . AMENITIES (nice things about house or location i.e. eat-in-kitchen, powder room, walk to railroad station, on a cul de sac.)

45 . . . ROOF MATERIAL (asphalt)

46 . . . WALL MATERIAL (Sheetrock)

47 . . . PARKING (attached garage)

48 . . . AIR-CONDITIONING (central)

49 . . . HEAT (hot water)

50 . . . FUEL (oil)

51 . . . GARBAGE PICKUP (private)

52 . . . ELECTRIC CO.

53 . . . WATER SUPPLIER (well or municipal)

54 . . . SEWER (septic)

55 . . . REMARKS (agents description)

56 . . . DIRECTIONS (to house)

AGENTS/AGENCIES

57 . . . LISTING DATE

58 . . . LISTING TYPE (exclusive or exclusive right to sell)

59 . . . NEGOTIATE THROUGH

60 . . . SUB-AGENT'S COMMISSION

61 . . . BUYER'S AGENT'S COMM.

62 . . . NAME OF OWNER

63 . . . OPEN HOUSE (date when house shown to agents)

64 . . . MODIFICATIONS/EXCLUSIONS (limitations on who will get paid, how, and when)

65 . . . LISTING OFFICE

66 . . . LISTING AGENT

67 . . . COOPERATING LISTING OFFICE

68 . . . COOPERATING LISTING AGENT

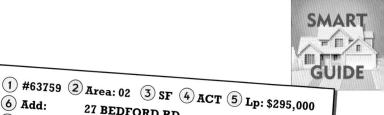

① #63759 ② Area: 02 ③ SF ④ ACT ⑤ Lp: $295,000
⑥ Add: 27 BEDFORD RD
⑦ PO: BAILEYVILLE   ZIP: 11111

⑧ Mun: BEDFORD FALLS
⑨ Rms:9 ⑩ Est.SF:2,800 ⑪ Sch:B1
⑫ Br:4 ⑮ Lr:18x12 ⑰ Es: Springfield
⑬ Bth:2   Jh: Jefferson
⑭ Lev:3 ⑯ Mbr:22x13   Hs: Ridgemont High

⑱ Styl:Col ⑲ Color: Grey ⑳ Att/Det: D
㉑ Modl: ㉒ Front:0 ㉓ Dep:0
㉔ Extr:Clap ㉕ Acre:0.55 ㉖ Shape:I
㉗ Yr Blt:1957
㉘ Home Asn:N ㉛ TX#:49-10-2-24
㉙ Nbhd Asn: N ㉜ EstTx$:8,340 ㉝ Tx Yr:97/98
㉚ Addl Fee: N ㉞ Asnt $: 60,000

㉟ L1: EH, LR, DR, EIK, FAM RM W/DR TO DECK,
㊱ L2: MBR W/BTH, 2 FAM BRS, HALL, HALL BATH,
㊲ L3: STUDY ㊳ Bsmt: FIN. LAUNDRY
㊴ Attic: STORAGE

㊵ POSS:ASAP ㊶ ZONING:R.5A

㊷ Includes: Rang, REF, DW, MICR
㊸ Excludes: WSHR, DRYR, WNDT
㊹ Amenities: EIK, PR, R.R., CUL SAC
㊺ Roof:ASPH ㊻ Walls: SROC
㊽ A/C Cent ㊼ Heat: HW ㊾ Parkg: AT-G 2CAR ㊿ Fuel: OIL
㊾ Heat: HW
㊿ Fuel: OIL
51 Garbage: PVT
52 Elec Co: NYSEG
53 Water: MUNI
54 Sewer: SEPT

55 Rems: IMMACULATE, CHARMING COL. HARDWOOD FLRS THROUGHOUT. DENTIL
MOLDINGS IN ALL RMS, CENT AC, PLAYRM & SITTING RM
ON LOWER LEVEL. PROFESSIONALLY LANDSCAPED. ON CUL DE SAC
56 Dir: DONNA REED LANE TO JIMMY STEWART RD.
HOUSE ON LEFT

57 LD: 08/24/97 58 LT:1A 59 Neg Thru: LA
60 Sub Agent %/$:3.0
61 Buyers Agent %/$:3.0

62 Owner: BLANDING
65 LO:Houlihan/Lawrence
67 CLO: NONE
64 Mod/Excl. X03 X04
66 LA:2801 Hutcheson, Libby
63 Open House: 09/12/ 97

68 CLA:NONE

REAL ESTATE AGENTS

The dormers (the dog-house like structures that project from the roof) tell you that this house is a Cape. Dormers are a clever way to add space and light to the second floor. They are especially useful when turning attics into living spaces.

PRICE GUIDELINES

What can you afford? Answer these two questions first: How much have you saved? (Lenders require 5 to 20 percent in cash for the down payment.) And how much do you make a year? Your yearly housing expenses shouldn't exceed 30 percent of your annual income. Housing expenses include your mortgage payments, property taxes, homeowners insurance, and utilities. Note: Don't forget to factor in closing costs, which can run from 2 to 7 percent of the home's purchase price. Ouch.

Who needs an agent? Most likely, you do. Why? Because most agents have access to the Multiple Listing Service (MLS), a computerized listing of all houses for sale in an area. Licensed agents can tap into the MLS to help buyers narrow their search. Conversely, when an agent lists your house on the MLS, it becomes available to that many more potential buyers.

If you want to *sell* your house, check out several real estate agencies; consider both local, privately-owned agencies and national franchises. Ask friends for referrals. When you've settled on an agency, you will sign a listing agreement; it usually lasts for up to six months. You'll be assigned to a listing agent who will: 1) help you set the price of the house; 2) advise you on ways to improve the look of your house; 3) create the spec sheet and promotional material; 4) arrange for your house to be shown. When your house is sold, you'll

pay a commission, usually between 5 and 7 percent. You can negotiate the amount. This commission is paid at the closing. It is then divided between the agency that brought the buyer and the agency that represented the seller.

If you would like to *buy* a house, these are the main things an agent will do for you: 1) provide you with spec sheets of suitable houses; 2) make appointments to show you houses and walk with you through them; 3) help you with bidding by telling you what comparable houses in the area have sold for; 4) arrange for a "binder"—a pre-contract agreement stipulating that the house can still be shown but other bids are contingent on yours falling through; 5) help arrange a home inspection; 6) recommend contractors to give you estimates on any necessary repairs; 7) relay your bid to the seller or the seller's agent; 8) assist in negotiating terms and dates of occupancy.

HOME BUYING
SMART

✔Work with an experienced agent. Agents are either buyer's agents, seller's agents, or dual-agents. Your needs as well as local practice will help determine your choice. Find out if your agent works full-time or part-time.

✔Know what you need, such as size and number of bedrooms. New, four-bedroom homes average 2,100 sq. ft. Don't waste your time or your agent's by looking at houses that are too small or too large.

✔Get a letter from a lender saying that based on your finances you qualify for a mortgage. This pre-approval can give you leverage when negotiating with the seller.

✔Location is everything. An average house on a great street will increase in value. A great house on an average or bleak street won't. Ask about schools, nearby transportation, local shopping, the neighborhood crime rate, and zoning regulations.

A "handyman's special" is a nickname for a house that needs a great deal of work, such as new wiring and plumbing. They are usually sold "as is." They can be great buys if you're handy.

 • You can sell a house without an agent and save on the commission, but it's a lot of work. You'll have to place ads in newspapers and be available to show your house.

• Write into the listing contract that you will pay the agent's commission when the title changes hands, not before. This protects you in case the sale falls through at the closing.

Stucco siding is weather-resistant and very durable. It is most commonly used in Tudor-style homes like this one, but it lends itself well to other styles.

 • Is the house in good shape? The house inspection will reveal problems, both real and potential. Note: Any house will need some work. If you're not handy or don't have the money to remodel, forget about buying a "handyman's special."

• Agent not working out? Buyers should go to another agency. Sellers should talk to the agency's managing broker and see if another agent can take over.

AGENT SOURCES

Century 21 800-446-8737

Coldwell Banker . . . 888-574-7653

ERA 800-798-8900

RE/MAX Int'l 800-525-7452

TRADE ASSOCIATION

National Association of Realtors 202-383-1000

INSPECTION

Before you sign a contract of sale, get the house inspected. If you cannot, put a home-inspection contingency clause in the contract. This will allow you to back out of the contract and get your deposit back should a subsequent inspection reveal unacceptable problems, whether they are structural or environmental.

The inspector's report will reveal potential problems—big and small—that the seller may not have disclosed or even known about. The findings can make or break a sale or prod the owner to lower the price of the house. Make sure you hire a qualified home inspector. Go through the house with the inspector to see exactly what he finds.

A housing inspector will visually check out a number of things: 1) signs of major exterior and interior damage; 2) condition of windows, doors, gutters, roof, basement; 3) functioning of major systems—heating, cooling, electrical, plumbing; and 4) signs of termite or other pest damage.

In the report, the inspector will cite each problem and evaluate its severity. Problems can range from major structural damage that cannot be easily fixed (i.e., termite-ridden support beams) to serious problems that are fixable (such as needing a new oil tank or septic tank), ending finally with standard wear-and-tear problems, such as broken window sashes or scuffed doors, that come with any "used" house.

ASBESTOS

TROUBLE From 1900 to 1970, this so-called miracle product of mineral fibers was used to insulate walls and pipes and strengthen vinyl floors and plaster walls. In the early '70s, it was found to cause cancer. Have suspect items found by the home inspector checked by an asbestos-testing agency. If the results are positive, you can have it removed. This must be done by professional asbestos removers. (Testing is fairly inexpensive; removal is not.) Or you can have it encapsulated by either covering it with a sealant or sealing it off with an airtight barrier. Note: Removing asbestos can be more hazardous than encapsulating it, and it must be disposed of correctly or you run the risk of a big fine.

Once the inspection is completed, the inspector will issue a report, typically a blend of a checklist and some comments, that details what is known and not known about the house. In older homes like this Victorian, expect numerous notations about wear and tear.

Houses in certain climates, like this Californian contemporary, have special home-inspection concerns, such as fire-retardant roof tiles and proper anchoring of the house to the foundation to withstand earthquakes.

and washed. Water-damaged carpets are unsightly and may have become moldy. Have them removed and the floors scrubbed down.

LEAD PAINT

Ingesting or breathing in high levels of lead paint through airborne paint dust can cause lead poisoning in adults and brain damage and stunted growth in children. Houses built before 1976 (the year lead paint was banned in the U.S.) could have lead in their interior or exterior paint. Have samples of paint tested. Over-the-counter testing kits are available at home center stores. To correct the problem, paint or wallpaper over it or remove it. Don't remove it yourself— that can be hazardous to your health.

TERMITES

Termites look like flying ants, but they don't fly very well. (They swarm every spring.) They live in soil and feed on wood by eating it from the inside out. A termite-eaten wooden beam, for instance, would be hollow. All houses, even newly constructed ones, should be inspected for termites by a licensed pest-control contractor. If inspection reveals termites, the house must be properly fumigated by a licensed exterminator. Typically, termite insecticide is injected into the soil where the termites live and is sometimes sprayed on areas where termite activity is suspected. Good news for buyers: the seller pays for getting rid of the termites.

Termite-damaged wood.

RADON GAS

It's an odorless, naturally occurring radioactive gas that is present to some degree in all soil. It can seep through the foundation into the basement. Exposure to high levels of radon may cause lung cancer. There are a number of low-priced over-the-counter house-screening tests for radon. If enough radon accumulates, you will need to cover any exposed earth with cement and have the basement and crawl spaces ventilated.

HOUSE ALLERGENS

House dust is a trigger for allergies and asthma. If the house is a mess, have it cleaned professionally. Check the air filter on the heating or cooling unit and change it often. Think about installing a nonallergic floor covering, such as tiles or linoleum. If you're allergic to pet hair, have walls and carpeting cleaned professionally. The heating and cooling system and vents should be vacuumed

INSPECTION RESOURCES

American Society of
Home Inspectors . . 800-743-2744

HouseMasters 800-526-3939

National Association of
Home Inspectors . . 800-448-3942

MORTGAGES

Ranches are single-level homes. Since they have no interior stairs, they are great for families with small children or people with mobility problems.

A split-level home has three levels of living space. The top floor is usually reserved for bedrooms, the middle level for kitchen and living room, and the bottom level, which is halfway underground, is for the family room or rec room.

Trying to get a mortgage is way up there on the stress monitor. Not only do you have to decide what type of mortgage you want before you apply for one, but you also have to shop around for the best interest rate. Then comes the really hard part: waiting for approval.

Just what are mortgages? Mortgages are loans made by lenders, such as mortgage companies, banks, and credit unions. Lenders use the prospective house or some other asset of yours as collateral. You can get a mortgage from mortgage companies, banks, or credit unions or you can hire a mortgage broker for a fee to shop the mortgage for you and hopefully find the best rate.

Once you've selected your lender, you will be asked to fill out a mortgage application and include with it such documents as past tax returns, recent pay stubs, employment history, and the house contract of sale. The lender will also check your credit history and do its own appraisal of the house, both of which you may pay for.

COMMON TYPES OF MORTGAGES

FIXED-RATE: same percentage rate charged over the life of the loan.

ADJUSTABLE-RATE: percentage rate may fluctuate throughout the year due to changes in key rate indexes.

FHA LOANS: government program that insures mortgages; minimal down payment is usually required.

CONSTRUCTION MORTGAGE: temporary financing used to build a new home or renovate an old one.

CLOSING

If applying for a mortgage is like applying to a college, then closing day is graduation. It is a formal gathering of the parties involved in the buying and selling of a house. All the work has been done—the property has been surveyed, the title has been searched and cleared, and the inspection prior to closing has been completed—it's now time to seal the deal.

Who is at the closing? It varies from state to state, but usually it's the seller and the buyer, their lawyers, the real estate agents, a representative of the title company, a representative of the lender, and, in some states, a closing or settlement agent who orchestrates the ritual. Yes, that's a lot of people sitting around a table talking.

What goes on? Again, closings vary from state to state, but usually it begins with the review and signing of key documents. The buyer signs the mortgage, the note, and other lender documents; the seller signs the deed and other transfer documents. Then the buyer, seller, and lender (or settlement agent) all sign the settlement sheet, or HUD-1, which is a list of closing costs and who pays them. Look that one over carefully.

When all documents are signed, dated, and notarized, the buyer hands over the certified checks. Fees and commissions are paid. Then, finally, the buyer gets the house keys in his or her hot little hands. (The deed is filed and recorded at the appropriate courthouse and then mailed to the new owner.) End of ritual—break open the champagne!

Raised ranches have two levels of living space, one "raised" above the other. The staircase in a raised ranch is split; the lower flight (which is halfway embedded in the ground) leads to the family room and garage, and the upper flight leads to the living area, kitchen, and bedrooms.

 CHECKLIST WHAT BUYERS NEED AT A CLOSING

✔ Proof of identity, such as a driver's license.

✔ Certified checks made payable to the appropriate parties. The biggest check covers the purchase price (less the mortgage) and your portion of the closing costs.

✔ Pens, a calculator, and your personal checkbook to pay for any minor adjustments for fuel, water, and taxes.

✔ A sense of humor. Buying or selling a home can be a big emotional milestone. Tears and nervous laughter are not uncommon. Note: Surprises (unexpected cost increases or decreases) can happen, but your lawyer should be able to handle it.

MORTGAGE RESOURCES

For the names of local lenders, call
Fannie Mae 800-732-6643

For the names of local mortgage brokers, call the National Association of Mortgage Brokers . . 703-610-0274

TRADESPEOPLE

Major jobs like adding a room or a wing, or converting a garage into an office (as shown in this Colonial), usually require the services of numerous tradespeople. It's best to have a general contractor coordinate their work.

Chances are, your house will need work or repairs done at some point and you'll need to call on tradespeople, namely electricians, plumbers, carpenters, tile setters, masons, drywallers, and roofers.

If the job is straightforward, then ask several general contractors (called a G.C. for short) to bid on it. G.C.s plan the work, file for building permits, order materials, and hire and supervise the tradespeople (sometimes called subcontractors).

If the job is complicated or you don't know what you want, hire an architect to put your dreams down on paper, then bid the job out to several G.C.s. It's good to have an architect if the job is complex or if you're solving problems. For an extra fee, an architect can make site visits to make sure the work is going according to plan.

Before you hire a tradesperson, G.C., or architect, make sure each one is accredited or licensed and has up-to-date insurance. Next, get references from previous clients. Contact the references and ask whether 1) the tradesperson and any assistants showed up on time; 2) kept to the cost estimate of the job; 3) worked on or supervised the job personally; 4) kept the job site safe; and 5) finished the job on time. If possible, ask to see the work that was done.

DRAWING UP A CONTRACT

CHECKLIST

✔ Define the scope of the work to be done in great detail. List types of material to be used and the brand names of any products.

✔ State when work is to begin and when it is to end. (If speed is of the essence, then note that payment will be jeopardized if the job is not finished by the specified date.)

✔ Write down a payment schedule. It should be tied to different stages of job completion—usually 10 to 30 percent down at signing, and the rest as the job progresses. The point is not to get too far ahead or behind the work. *WARNING:* If a contractor asks for more than 30 percent at signing, question it immediately.

✔ Hold the last payment back until all work is done and inspected and the G.C. and all tradespeople have signed a release of lien stating that all their payments have been made to suppliers and other tradespeople. That way they can't file a mechanic's lien on your house for work and materials you've already paid for.

✔ List under what circumstances the agreement can be terminated, such as dissatisfaction with quality or progress of work. State whether disputes will be taken to civil court or to arbitration. (Arbitration is speedier and less costly.)

SHORTCUTS

• Save money and be your own G.C. Coordinating the work of different tradespeople is a full-time job, but it can save money. Don't do it unless you know about construction and housing regulations; otherwise, you might pay more in the long run.

• Hire an architect for a few hours of consultation. Such advice and expertise can help provide ingenious solutions to a problem.

TRADE RESOURCES

American Arbitration
Assoc. 800-778-7879

American Institute
of Architects. 800-242-9930

National Assoc. of
Home Builders 202-822-0216

National Association of
Plumbing, Heating and Cooling
Contractors 800-533-7694

National Assoc. of the
Remodeling Ind. . . . 800-440-6274

CONTRACT REVIEWERS

American Homeowners
Foundation. 703-536-7776

Smart Consumer
Services 703-416-0257

United Homeowners
Assoc. 202-408-8842

New houses, such as this postmodern contemporary, often need work after they have settled in their foundation. Postmodern homes mix classical architectural elements (columns, half-round windows) to make contemporary homes look less austere.

IMPROVEMENTS

Before making any kind of internal repairs or improvements to your home that are not strictly cosmetic, you need to call your local building department and find out what is allowed, if permits are required, and if licensed tradespeople must do the work. Plan ahead—obtaining permits takes time, and you may have to submit architectural drawings and an engineer's report before you get them.

In most communities, you'll need a building permit for such things as renovating a kitchen or bath, converting a basement, garage, or attic into living quarters, enclosing a porch or patio, installing a new electrical system, replacing a heating system, building an exterior retaining wall more than 4' high, building a barbecue with a chimney more than 6' high, breaking through a curb to install a driveway, drilling a well, or installing a pool.

If local building regulations do not allow your project, you can apply for a variance from your local zoning board. Zoning ordinances cover the size and shape of a home and how close it can be to either the road or your neighbors. They will certainly affect any additions you have in mind. Find out exactly what the rules and regulations are in your community before you begin work, or you may find yourself paying a big fine or, worse, having to tear down what you've built.

Building codes set minimum safety standards for things like exits, fire protection, light and ventilation, bathrooms, and energy conservation. Code requirements vary not only across the country but often between neighboring communities. All jobs that necessitate a permit will have an official inspector to come and approve the work during and after completion.

Town houses usually come with bylaws and covenants—rules that the community owners must adhere to or face penalties.

Tudors combine stucco, wood, and brick; their high-pitched roofs are good for snowy climates.

SPECIAL NEEDS

 The Americans with Disabilities Act (ADA) requires commercial buildings to be accessible to people with disabilities. Private homes are exempt from meeting these requirements. However, as none of us is getting any younger, it might be a good idea to make our homes easier and safer to move around in. Note: The average wheelchair is 27" wide.

✔ Doors and stairs: Exterior doors should be 36" wide. Install ramps that rise no more than 1" for every 12" of its length. Minimum width for an interior door, when open, is 32" (36" is better). Eliminate threshold molding. Replace doorknobs with lever handles.

✔ Kitchen: Countertops should be 32"–34" from the floor; lower the upper cabinets to 15" above the countertop; use sliding or swing-out compartments in lower and upper cabinets for easier access. The sink should be no higher than 34" above the floor (with a sink depth of no more than 6½"). Leave empty space beneath the sink for knees. The cooktop should have controls in front.

✔ Hallways and light switches: Hallways need to be 36"–48" wide. Light switches should be no higher than 50" above the floor.

✔ Flooring: Use dense, low-pile carpet glued directly to the floor.

✔ Bathroom: Allow a minimum 30" x 48" clear floor space for each fixture; the sink should be 34" from the floor. Install single-lever faucets and a handheld showerhead; get a fold-up seat for the shower stall and tub; anchor grab bars into the walls beside the toilet, tub, and shower.

SPECIAL NEEDS SOURCES

Access with Ease. . . 520-636-9469 (catalog)

adaptAbility . . . . 800-243-9232 (catalog)

Council of American Building Officials . . . 703-931-4533

Eastern Paralyzed Veterans Assoc. 718-803-3782

MOVING

Mediterranean-style homes have tiled roofs and stucco siding. Both are fire-retardant materials, making this style very popular in hot, dry climates.

Moving smart takes planning. If you are moving a great distance, better hire professional interstate movers. Get bids on the cost of your move from two or three movers. A representative of the moving company will come to look at the amount of stuff you are moving. They will base their estimates on the number of pounds shipped. The minimum weight required by interstate movers is 1,000 pounds; the average household is 6,000 pounds. Be prepared to pay extra if there are stairs, elevators, long entranceways, or narrow streets to contend with at either end of the move.

Compare the estimates and decide on a mover. The moving company will draw up a contract and set a moving date. After your goods are packed and on board, the truck will be weighed and the company will let you know the exact amount of money due upon delivery. Check your homeowners insurance to see if it covers items lost or damaged during a move. Note: A moving company's "valuation protection" covers only what it packs, so have the movers pack all breakable items.

When the truck arrives at your new house, the driver will give you an itemized list of your goods. Check off each item. If anything is missing, or is broken, note it on the form. Don't worry about unpacking to check for broken items in boxes right away; depending on your agreement, you may have up to 270 days to file a loss or damage claim. (Leave broken pieces in the packing box as proof.) After you've checked everything off, you will then pay the driver with a money order or traveler's checks. Tipping is appreciated—let the driver distribute it to the crew.

CHECKLIST MOVING SMART ✔Get change-of-address cards from the post office. Obtain copies of records from doctors, dentists, and schools. Arrange to have utilities and phone service canceled the day *after* you move.

✔Assemble packing tools, such as scissors, tape, bubble wrap, labels, pens, and utility knife in a plastic hamper to speed packing.

✔Work backward and pack stuff you don't need first (books and knickknacks); pack important items last (cooking utensils, dishes, towels, and linens).

✔Color code boxes with colored stickers or colored markers—for example, green for the living room, red for the kitchen.

✔Don't pack jewelry and important documents in boxes. Put them in their own suitcase and take it with you when you leave.

✔Put enough clothing, sheets, towels, and toiletries for a week in suitcases and take them with you. Include a few of your kids' favorite toys, games, books, or videos.

✔Disconnect appliances you are moving correctly; call the manufacturer if you're not sure how. (Note: Some movers are not allowed to disconnect appliances.) Also make sure appliances are clean and dry inside.

✔Empty gas and oil from yard equipment.

✔Gather up critical unpacking items (scissors, tape, soap, paper towels, cleansers, trash bags, shelf liner, paper plates and cups) in your packing hamper and pack it in a specially marked box.

✔Unpack the kids' rooms first or set up a play area for them. If possible, arrange for a babysitter. Then tackle the kitchen, the bathrooms, and the other bedrooms.

Most moves usually take place in summer. You—not the movers— should take all items that might be damaged in a hot truck (cassettes, CDs, records, and computer disks).

 SHORTCUTS • The IRS will allow you to deduct the cost of a job-related move of at least 60 miles from your previous home. Keep records and receipts of all move-related expenses.

• Save money and move yourself. Rental trucks are priced by the number of cubic feet they hold. When in doubt, go for a bigger size. Load large things first, starting from the bottom and working up. Secure drawers, and stand mattresses upright. Rent cloth pads (to help cushion furniture) and a dolly.

MOVERS

Allied	800-470-2851
Atlas Van Lines	800-638-9797
Mayflower	800-428-1200
United Van Lines	800-948-4885

TRUCK RENTALS

Penske	800-222-0277
Ryder	800-467-9337
U-Haul	800-528-0463

GET HOUSE SMART

FORMAL ROOMS

The foyer, dining room, and living room are the so-called formal rooms. In older houses these rooms were used solely for greeting and entertaining, so they had all the fancy furniture, elegant flooring, and snazzy decorations. How formal do you want to be? Read on and decide.

FORMAL ROOMS

The most elaborate architectural details in a house are usually found in the living room, dining room, foyer, and main stairway. The number guide will help you identify the parts of these rooms. Detailed explanations follow in the chapter.

PAINT

1 . . . EGGSHELL PAINT

2 . . . SEMIGLOSS PAINT

MOLDINGS

3 . . . BASEBOARD

4 . . . BASE SHOE

5 . . . CROWN MOLDING

DOOR/WINDOW

6 . . . DOOR CASING

7 . . . WINDOW CASING

8 . . . MUNTIN

9 . . . DEAD-BOLT LOCK

10 . . . DOORKNOB

FLOORS

11 . . . HARDWOOD

12 . . . MARBLE TILE

LIGHTING

13 . . . TORCHIERE

14 . . . TABLE LAMP

STAIRS

15 . . . RISER

16 . . . TREAD

17 . . . HANDRAIL

18 . . . BALUSTER

19 . . . NEWEL POST/PILLAR

FLOORS

There's a classic beauty to hardwood floors, and it can have a powerful effect on the mood and tone of a room. To emphasize its simple beauty choose a stain that complements your decor.

Many houses are built with pine or oak floors. If the wood shows only minor scratches here and there, have the floor professionally sanded and finished with either a natural stain or a color pigment. Then seal it with a good-quality polyurethane or varnish. The floor will be in good shape for 5–10 years, depending on foot traffic.

If the wood floors are deeply stained, pitted, or scarred, you can cover them with ceramic tile (see page 114), vinyl tile (see page 116), or carpet (see page 86). Or to retain the same warmth and elegance, you can replace them with new hardwood flooring.

Hardwood flooring comes in various configurations: 1) tongue-and-groove strips, 1½"–2½" wide, that conceal nails; 2) Planks 3"–8" wide, either newly manufactured or reclaimed from old houses and barns; and 3) parquet, tile-like pieces of wood arranged in a pattern of alternating grains.

Once wood flooring is installed, it is treated with a stain and/or sealed with polyurethane or varnish. Good news: Laminated wood flooring is a new type of prefinished wood covering, so there's no sanding or staining after installation.

TIME FACTOR	
INSTALL	**FLOORER'S TIME**
Oak floor (12' × 12')	6 hrs
Parquet floor (12' × 12')	6 hrs
NOTE: Plus 2 hours to sand, 1 hour to seal, and 24 hours to cure	

• An unsightly scratch? Lightly sand the scratch with sandpaper until it disappears, then apply finish to match the rest of the floor. Deeper scratches and gouges require expert repair; call in a professional.

• Worn thresholds? New floors call for new thresholds—wood or marble strips, 2"–4" wide, that fit across most doorways. Have the old ones pulled up and replaced.

Ceramic-tile floors are especially good for entrance halls, which receive the heaviest traffic in the house.

Vinyl tile is easy to install and is available in a slew of colors and patterns.

Parquet is the French word for geometrically patterned wood. It is installed square by square, like ceramic tile. The squares come in many different types of wood, some of them already composed into patterns.

HARDWOOD-FLOORING SOURCES

Anderson
Hardwood 864-833-6250

Bruce Hardwood. . . 800-722-4647

Harris-Tarkett. 800-842-7816

Historic Floors
of Oshkosh 920-582-9977

Mannington Wood
Floors 800-814-7355

LIGHTING

Lighting your formal rooms will be harder than you think. Why? Because a light fixture must not only provide the right amount of light, it must also match the style of the room. Getting both right is not always easy.

Here are some basics. Lighting falls into two groups: indirect (ambient) and direct (accent and task). The former sets the mood, the latter spotlights centers of interest or focuses on work surfaces. Chandeliers can be good sources of indirect light. They can also create the illusion of more space. Track, pendant, and recessed ceiling lights can give off light that is more direct, (see page 56).

Wall sconces are good choices where space is tight. There are two types of sconces: downlights, which direct the light down to the floor, and uplights, which throw light up, reflecting it off the ceiling. In general, downlights act as direct lighting, especially along hallways and stairs, and uplights lend ambient light for background illumination.

TIME FACTOR	
INSTALL	ELECTRICIAN'S TIME
Chandelier	2 hrs
Pendant light	1 hr
Recessed light	½ hr
Track light	1 hr
Wall sconce	½ hr

Chandeliers are good for general lighting, but the shades on this one help focus the light on the table. The amount of light can be regulated with a dimmer.

Standing lights, or torchieres, provide excellent uplighting (above). They stand at about 6', the same height as sconces, but do not have to be mounted. Many torchieres are made for halogen bulbs, but because of the heat they give off they should not be placed near curtains or other flammable material.

Wall sconces add architectural detail to a room and can emit a soft, indirect glow along a wall, but consider before installing them—they will highlight any unsightly flaws in the wall or ceiling.

 LIGHTING SMART

CHECKLIST

✔ Figure out how much light you need. The rule of thumb is to have one watt of light for every square foot (double that for kitchens and work areas).

✔ For safety's sake, pay attention to the wattage limits on lamps and other fixtures.

✔ Buy fixtures close to home. Finding the right fixture usually involves trial and error. To save time returning fixtures, shop locally.

✔ Make sure the fixture will fit the mounting waiting for it back home. (Some sconces, for instance, require the installation of a special mounting plate.)

✔ Halogen bulbs emit a pure white light, and they last longer than incandescent bulbs while using less wattage. However, they generate a great deal of heat; they can be a potential hazard if the bulb comes in contact with curtains, papers, or bedding.

✔ Check that every lamp or fixture has passed a UL (Underwriters Laboratories) inspection. If there is no UL label, don't buy it.

SHORTCUTS

• Save on the hassle of installing ceiling lights by using floor lamps for ambient light instead.

• Stop fumbling in the dark for the switch on a lamp. Have an electrician connect the lamp outlet to a wall switch by the door so you can flick it on as you enter the room.

• New energy savers are compact fluorescent light bulbs.

LIGHTING FIXTURE SOURCES

Cooper Lighting. . . . 847-501-5455

Juno Lighting 800-367-5866

Lightolier 800-223-0726

Thomas Lighting . . . 800-365-4448

Underwriters Laboratories. 847-272-8800

DRYWALL

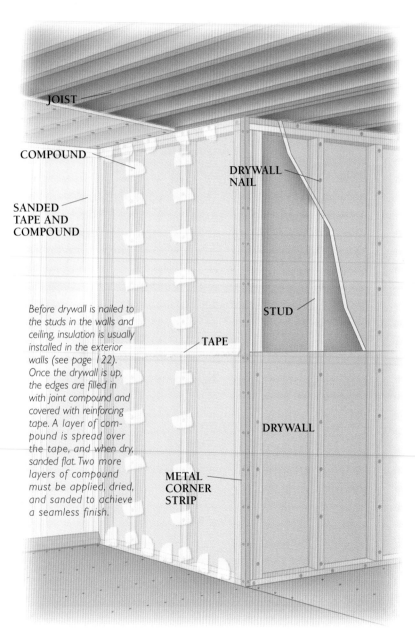

JOIST

COMPOUND

SANDED TAPE AND COMPOUND

DRYWALL NAIL

Before drywall is nailed to the studs in the walls and ceiling, insulation is usually installed in the exterior walls (see page 122). Once the drywall is up, the edges are filled in with joint compound and covered with reinforcing tape. A layer of compound is spread over the tape, and when dry, sanded flat. Two more layers of compound must be applied, dried, and sanded to achieve a seamless finish.

STUD

TAPE

DRYWALL

METAL CORNER STRIP

Before you can paint, wallpaper, or panel, you really need to know what that stuff is underneath it all. The walls in new houses are nearly always surfaced with drywall.

What's drywall? It is compressed gypsum (a chalky substance that comes from rocks) encased in heavy paper. Drywall, also known as Sheetrock panels or wallboard comes in 4' x 6' (or larger) panels that can be ½" to ⅝" thick. The thicker the drywall, the stronger it is. There are three types of drywall: 1) regular (for general applications); 2) fire-resistant (for use where fire hazards are acute, especially around heaters); and 3) water-resistant (for damp and humid areas). However, for walls that are directly exposed to water, such as shower stalls and bath surrounds, use super-water-resistant cement board.

Plaster walls are found in older homes. Plaster provides better insulation and soundproofing than drywall. And it is also takes wear and tear better.

TIME FACTOR

DRYWALL	DRYWALL CONTRACTOR'S TIME
Hang drywall	3 hrs
Fill coat & tape	5 hrs
Sanding	1 hr

NOTE: Estimates are for 12' x 12' room, and do not include drying time.

HANGING PICTURES

In the best of all possible worlds, you should nail picture fasteners directly into studs. Locate them by rapping the wall (a thudding sound indicates a stud; a hollow sound signals a space between them). Or run a magnet over the wall to find the nails in the studs. If you can't locate a stud or if it's not in the right location, try drywall fasteners. To support a light-weight item, such as a small picture frame that weighs less than 10 lbs., a spiral anchor screws easily into the drywall. Or

Spiral anchor

Drive anchor

you can install a drive anchor which has a small bolt fitted into a threaded sleeve. For a heavier item—a big wall clock, for example—a molly bolt or a toggle fastener works best. Inserted in a pre-drilled hole, their flanges expand to grip the back of the wall.

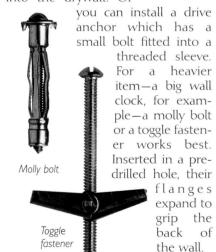

Molly bolt

Toggle fastener

Drywall is easily dented. Treat it kindly, and repair dings with compound and careful sanding.

 TROUBLE • Small gouges and cracks? You can fix them yourself. Add a thin layer of compound and smooth with a straight edge. Allow to dry, then sand and repeat with another layer of compound. Sand again, wipe off the dust, then paint.

• Drywall nail popping out? Call in a handyperson who will remove the offending nail and replace it with a drywall screw, then spackle over the screw and let it dry. Sand the spackle, then paint.

• Doorknob bumping into the drywall? Install a doorstop to protect the wall from the constant impact.

DRYWALL SOURCES

American Gypsum. . 800-545-6302

Georgia Pacific. 800-225-6119

National Gypsum. . . 800-628-4662

USG Corp.. 800-874-4968

PAINT

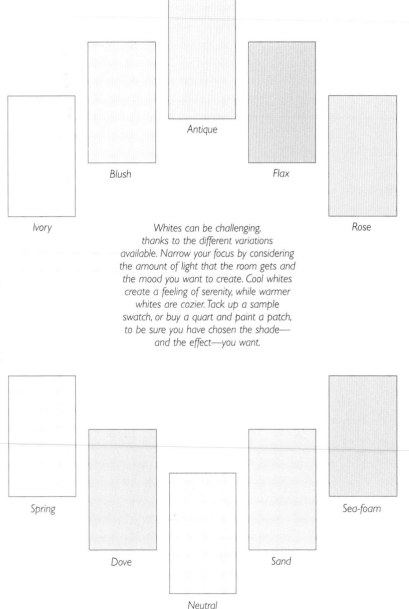

Ivory

Blush

Antique

Flax

Rose

Whites can be challenging, thanks to the different variations available. Narrow your focus by considering the amount of light that the room gets and the mood you want to create. Cool whites create a feeling of serenity, while warmer whites are cozier. Tack up a sample swatch, or buy a quart and paint a patch, to be sure you have chosen the shade— and the effect—you want.

Spring

Dove

Neutral

Sand

Sea-foam

Just forget about color for just a minute. Think first about the kind of wear a painted surface will get. The more wear that's expected, the more "washable" the paint must be. There are two basic types of interior paints: water-based (latex) and oil-based (alkyd). Latex has little odor and dries faster, but alkyd paint has higher "washability."

Both types of paints come in different lusters, or sheens. Gloss paint is very shiny; it has high washability, but it reveals imperfections in a wall and shows brushstrokes if not applied carefully; it is excellent for trim. Semigloss paint is fairly washable, but less shiny; it's good for kitchens and baths. Eggshell (or satin) paint has little sheen and some washability, and shows few imperfections; it's good for formal and family rooms. Flat paint has no sheen and is the least washable; use it on ceilings and for walls in living rooms, dining rooms, and bedrooms.

Okay, now you can consider color. Most hardware stores and home centers offer paint charts and swatches. Light reflects differently off each wall in a room, so tack up swatches in several different places. Watch the effect of changing light before choosing a color.

PAINT MATH

A gallon of paint covers about 400 sq. ft. of primed surface. To figure out a room's square footage, multiply the length of each wall by the height, then add all the numbers together. For the ceiling, multiply the length and width of the floor. Get extra paint for applying bright colors, or for covering sheens.

To make a room appear bigger and less boxy-looking, paint the ceiling and trim a brighter white than the walls.

SHORTCUTS • Wrap paint-laden rollers and brushes tightly in several layers of plastic wrap. Make sure both ends are sealed shut. This will keep them moist and ready for use overnight, or for days, if a painting job is interrupted.

• Save some paint in a small, tight-lidded jar and keep it in a handy place for quick touch-ups.

TROUBLE • Bubbles or blistering paint? These are signs that moisture is seeping in under the paint. Check for leaks in the walls and ceilings and correct. If no leaks are found, then the surface was probably not properly prepared. Call the painter and have it redone.

• Lead paint? In a pre-1980s house peeling or flaking lead-based paint poses a health hazard. Get a testing kit and sample a chip. If it's leaded, call in an expert to seal or remove it (see page 13).

PAINT SOURCES

Benjamin Moore . . . 800-826-2623

DULUX
(Glidden) 800-663-8589

Pratt & Lambert . . . 800-289-7728

PPG Industries
(Lucite). 800-441-9695

Sherwin-Williams
(Dutch Boy). 800-828-5669

CHECKLIST PAINTING SMART

✔ Remove anything hanging on the walls, as well as the curtains and shades. Unscrew switch and outlet plates. Cover ceiling fixtures with plastic. Move the furniture to the center of the room and drape it with plastic. Roll up area rugs. Cover the floor or carpet with a heavy drop cloth.

✔ Repair any cracks and nail holes in the walls with spackling compound; for woodwork, use wood putty. Sand smooth.

✔ Wash baseboards, window sills, and trim thoroughly to clean them and dull their finish so paint will adhere well. Allow to dry.

✔ Use a roller for large, flat surfaces, and a brush or sponge pad for woodwork and edging. Stir the paint and pour it into a smaller container or a roller tray.

✔ Paint from the ceiling down, painting the flat surfaces first, then the woodwork and trim.

✔ Wipe up any spills quickly.

✔ Rinse brushes and rollers in warm sudsy water (for latex paint) or solvent (for alkyd paint). Wash the roller tray as well and set it upside down to dry.

✔ Admire your handywork.

MOLDINGS

Ceiling molding and baseboards lend classy decorative detail to a room. Better still, they hide gaps and cracks caused by settling. Chair rails protect walls from being scuffed by furniture. All of these moldings can be made from softwoods (pine, poplar) or hardwoods (oak, mahogany) or wood veneer and plastic. Use softwoods if you plan to paint the moldings; use hardwoods if you plan to stain them and want the grain of the wood to show.

Most baseboard moldings are made of wood that is 3"–5" wide and tapered at the top. A rounded, narrow molding called a base shoe or quarter-round trim is usually attached to the base of the baseboard to hide any gaps between the baseboard and floor. Baseboards are nailed into the walls with finishing nails (nails with small heads that can be sunk into the wood).

Ceiling moldings and crown moldings are placed near where the wall meets the ceiling. Choose from cap, crown, or cove molding styles. Ornate patterns are available in lightweight plastics for easier hanging, but wood is more common.

A chair rail is placed at the height of the back of a dining room chair—about one-third of the wall height from the floor. It's an effective way to set off a dining area from a living room. Paint it the same color as the door moldings or choose a shade that complements the color of the wall.

Molding should match the style and period of the house. If you have an older home and want to add molding, look for styles that are similar to the door and window casings, that are already there.

Crown
moldings

Baseboard
moldings

Ornate
dentil
ceiling trim

Chair rail

Decorative chair rail or ceiling trim

 SHORTCUTS
• Ceiling molding is best used in rooms with high ceilings; it can make rooms with low ceilings feel cramped. The bigger the room, the wider and more ornate the molding can be.

• To set off a chandelier or a droplight, install a circular molding, called a medallion, around it. Available in lightweight plastic, medallions can be painted to match the rest of the trim.

• Stained or varnished baseboards usually hide nicks better than painted ones do.

TROUBLE
• Gaps in the molding? Like all wood, molding contracts and expands when the weather changes. Fill slight gaps with paintable caulk; it is elastic enough to contract and expand with the wood.

WAINSCOTING

Traditional wainscoting is made from paneling or tongue-and-groove planking that is fitted together and hung vertically, starting underneath the baseboard and going a third of the way up the wall. It is usually trimmed with a chair rail along the top. Wainscoting is an attractive way to protect the wall. Convenient ready-made panels make quick work of installation.

Embossed
wallpaper borders

MOLDING SOURCES

Architectural
Products 800-835-4400

Sierra Pacific Ind. 916-378-8000
Local lumber yards or
local home centers . . .(see page 4)

STAIRS

Stairs are perhaps the most dangerous part of your house. For that reason, they are often encumbered with numerous strict building-code requirements. Stairs in older homes probably won't be up to code, but you can remedy that by adding safety improvements such as double railing, or carpeting for the treads.

First, stair vocabulary. Stringers are the long, diagonal, sawtooth pieces that support the stairs. Treads, the horizontal planks that run across the stringers, are the parts you step on, and risers are the vertical parts that rise (get it?) from one tread to the next. Then come the support structures, namely: the railing (or handrail), which is attached to the wall with metal brackets or sits on those vertical spindles (called balusters). The large, decorative post that anchors the bottom (and sometimes the top) of the railing is called the newel post.

Most good lumberyards have a vast array of railing and baluster styles ranging from the stark utilitarian to the sweepingly grand. Most of them are available in several types of wood or in metal. You can even purchase a fancy new newel post.

To save space, old houses typically have very high risers and narrow treads, which can make them treacherous to climb. Building codes today say that new risers should be no higher than 8" and treads should be at least 10" wide. Make older stairs safer by adding a handrail along the wall, installing slip-resistant material on the treads, and lighting the staircase well.

CHECKLIST — CARPETING THE STAIRS

✔ For safety's sake, consider carpeting your stairs. This is all but mandatory if there will be small children in your house.

✔ Look for carpet that is high in density and twist (see page 86). Industrial-grade carpeting with a pattern is ideal.

✔ Choose good-quality padding. Your carpet will last longer.

✔ The stairs will need to be measured; this is usually done by an expert from the carpet store. If you prefer a runner, the carpet will be cut and its edges bound so they won't unravel.

✔ Decide how you want the carpet to be installed: it can either cascade down over the lip of the stair treads to cover the riser (called a "waterfall") or it can be fitted and tacked over each tread to form a neat round edge (called "capping").

TROUBLE

• Squeaky step? Call the carpenter. If the squeak is at the front end of the step, it can be eliminated by hammering a finishing nail at an angle through the step into the riser below it. If the squeak is toward the back, then a slim piece of wood (a shim) is inserted between the tread and the riser above it.

• Loose balusters? These can be secured by wedging a thin piece of wood into the top of the baluster. If that doesn't work, a finishing nail needs to be put in at an angle up through the top edge of the ballister into the handrail. Call the carpenter.

• Safety worries? In older homes, staircases can be quite wide. If there is no second railing on the wall side of the stairs, have one installed.

TIME FACTOR

INSTALL	CARPENTER'S TIME
Staircase kit	1 day
Spiral Stair Kit	1 day
Pre-fab Spiral Staircase	2 hrs

REPAIR	CARPENTER'S TIME
Broken tread	½ hr
Baluster	½ hr

STAIR SOURCES

A.J. Stairs 800-425-7824

The Iron Shop 800-523-7427

L.J. Smith Stair
System, Inc. 614-269-2221

Stairways, Inc. 800-231-0793

Taney Corp. 410-756-6671

Spiral staircases with open risers are an effective way to conserve space without blocking light. They can be purchased in kit form.

KITCHEN

I t's still command central, but thanks to new kitchen designs it can also be a living room where you entertain and relax, and oh, yes, cook. To make your kitchen this user-friendly, read on.

KITCHEN

To get kitchen smart, use this easy number guide to identify and name all the parts of your kitchen. Detailed explanations follow in the chapter.

CABINETS

1 . . . UPPER

2 . . . BASE

3 . . . DOOR PULL

4 . . . OPEN SHELVING

5 . . . DRAWER

6 . . . DRAWER PULL

7 . . . TOE KICK or KICK PLATE

COUNTERTOP

8 . . . SURFACE

9 . . . EDGE or BULLNOSE

10 . . . BACKSPLASH

SINK

11 . . . SELF-RIMMING DOUBLE BASINS

12 . . . BUILT-IN DRAINBOARD

13 . . . FAUCET

14 . . . SPRAYER

15 . . . SINK RIM

16 . . . DISPOSAL (not seen)

DISHWASHER

17 . . . PUSH-BUTTON CONTROLS

TRASH COMPACTOR

18 . . . PUSH-BUTTON CONTROLS

REFRIGERATOR

19 . . . SIDE-BY-SIDE

20 . . . ICE/WATER DISPENSER

21 . . . CONDENSER COILS (behind grill)

STOVE/OVEN

22 . . . ELECTRIC COOKTOP (built-in)

23 . . . AIR DUCTS (not seen)

24 . . . OVEN (built-in)

25 . . . CONVECTION/ MICROWAVE OVEN

26 . . . RECIRCULATING VENT

27 . . . MICROWAVE OVEN

LIGHTING

28 . . . FLUORESCENT TASK LIGHTING (not seen)

29 . . . UNDER-CABINET LIGHTING

30 . . . GFCI (not seen)

FLOORS/WALLS

31 . . . SEMIGLOSS PAINT

32 . . . VINYL WALL COVERING

33 . . . VINYL TILE

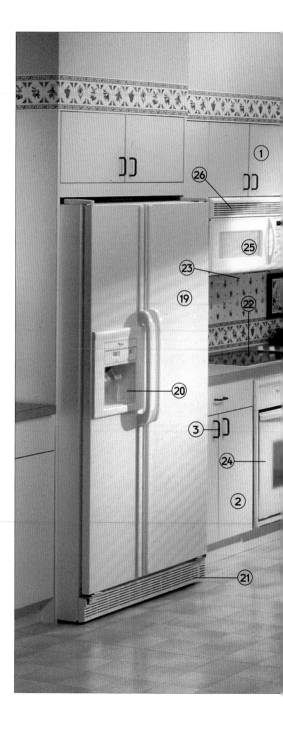

PLANNING

MINIMUM CLEARANCES FOR THE L-SHAPED KITCHEN

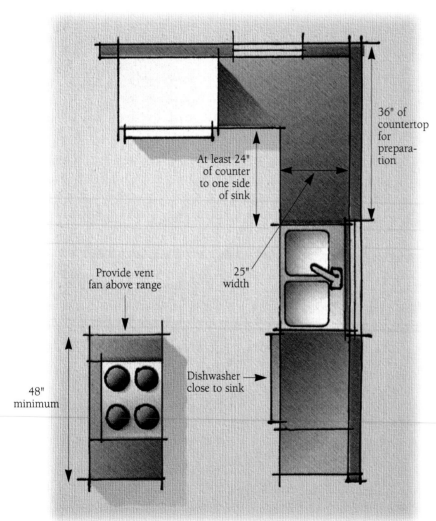

36" of countertop for preparation

At least 24" of counter to one side of sink

Provide vent fan above range

25" width

48" minimum

Dishwasher close to sink

Nothing adds to the value of your house like a smart, attractive kitchen where the parts all work in sync. Whether you're starting from scratch, renovating, or working on just a section, plan it well. For starters, note what you lack in your current kitchen. Do you need more counterspace? Would you like a desk? Do your cooking appliances fit your needs? Is there more than one cook in the house? How's the lighting? And what can you afford to spend? Your answers—and those of other family members—will help shape your planning.

The old thinking: work triangles. The new thinking: work centers. The difference? With work triangles, the sink, stove, and refrigerator form a triangle. With work centers, you can create a workstation wherever there is enough counter space next to a major appliance or a sink. An island or a peninsula can provide several small workstations, or one large one. The benefits of work centers? A center-based layout is both efficient and flexible, especially for families with more than one cook.

KITCHEN DO'S AND DONT'S

✔ An average kitchen measures about 150 sq. ft. and has about 10 sq. ft. of counter space around the sink and stove. If you need a larger area, try appropriating square footage from an adjoining room, closet, or hallway. Capture wall space by relocating a doorway or window. Or build cabinets right up to the ceiling to create out-of-the way storage for items that are not used that often.

MINIMUM CLEARANCES FOR THE U-SHAPED KITCHEN

If used as a breakfast area allow 24" for each person

Walkway 36" minimum

15" minimum counterspace on latch side of refrigerator

24" of counter to one side of sink

THE GALLEY KITCHEN

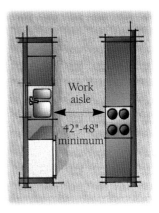

Work aisle

42"-48" minimum

Kitchen renovations can take anywhere from two weeks for a small kitchen to three months for a large one. They usually require a building permit. Check with your local building department.

✔ Check out home centers for advice on kitchen design. Some home centers will create a computer-generated model for you.

✔ Major appliances used for surface cooking must have fans or vents to circulate air or ducted to the outside.

✔ Save counterspace and hang a microwave oven from an upper cabinet.

✔ Good lighting is one of the keys to good cooking. The simplest plans use recessed ceiling and undercounter lights to highlight countertops, stove, and sink and a pendant light over the kitchen table.

✔ Be sure to have at least two waste receptacles; one for garbage and at least one other for recyclables.

✔ Install a fire extinguisher near an exit (and away from cooking equipment).

✔ Make your kitchen wheelchair-friendly. (See page 19 for resources.) Entryways need to be at least 32" wide. To better use the sink, remove the base cabinet in which the sink sits so that the wheelchair user's knees can fit underneath. To access freezer space, get either a refrigerator with the freezer on the bottom or a side-by-side model.

KITCHEN RESOURCES

National Kitchen & Bath Assoc. 800-843-6522

National Assoc. of the Remodeling Industry 800-440-6274

CABINETS

On the European-style cabinets above, the doors are frameless and have concealed hinges. The doors and drawers abut each other to form a sleek, smooth surface.

Brace yourself: cabinets are pretty pricey. Upper cabinets are usually less expensive than the larger base cabinets. The higher the quality of the cabinet, the more expensive.

Stock cabinets are manufactured according to standard sizes. Starting at 9" wide, they increase by 3" increments to a maximum of 48" wide. You can mix and match widths to achieve a custom fit and to accommodate appliances. Always check appliance widths and heights when measuring for cabinets.

Before you decide on style or color, consider the look. Do you want traditional or European? Traditional cabinets have "face-frames"—the edges of the cabinets are covered with frames of finished wood that are visible around the doors, and the hinges can be seen. European cabinets have no face frames and the hinges can't be seen, resulting in a more contemporary look.

Feeling guilty about trashing your old cabinets? Don't replace, reface. Leave the old cabinets and just put new doors and drawer fronts on them. Cover the front edges and other visible surfaces with matching wood veneer. Refacing works if old cabinets are in good condition, and costs about the same as a new set of uninstalled, medium-quality cabinets.

TIME FACTOR

INSTALL	CARPENTER'S TIME
8 new cabinets (plus 1 day to rip out the old)	1 day
Reface 8 cabinets	3 days

QUICK QUALITY CHECKS

✔Most cabinet sides are made of veneer glued over particleboard panels that are ⅝" to ¾" thick. (Less expensive cabinets use ½" or ⁹⁄₁₆".) Push on the side of the cabinet. If it's poorly made, you'll feel it buckle.

✔Look for drawer sides made of solid wood (not particleboard) and gap-free joinery. If the joints are held together by nails and glue, walk away. Likewise, if the drawer doesn't stay rigid when you remove it and push it corner to corner, keep shopping.

✔Drawers should fit solidly and slide smoothly. There should be no side-to-side movement when they are fully extended.

✔Shelves should sit on hefty metal clips— not plastic ones. The minimum thickness for a shelf in a 36" cabinet is ¾", (⅝"-thick shelves will do in narrower units).

•Damaged cabinet door? If you can't replace it with an exact match, consider installing a louvered (slatted) or decorative glass door. Or leave the door off entirely to create open shelving.

•Mysterious dampness or odors? Minor plumbing leaks may have gone unnoticed for years behind or beneath cabinets. Have a plumber check for them.

•Gouges in countertops? Be sure to repair any damage where water can seep through.

Many custom and high-end stock face-frame cabinets (right) are made like fine furniture, with fully inset doors that fit snugly within the frame.

CABINETS

Cathedral-style raised panel door

Frame and panel door

Frame and panel door with batten

Glass panel door

European-style laminate door

Clear a place to organize your household by "borrowing" counter space for a built-in desk. Make sure there's room for a computer, phone, and maybe even a few cookbooks.

Cabinet doors give a kitchen much of its character. Your choices of material and edging trim come down to this: solid wood, wood veneer, laminated particleboard, and melamine (a type of plastic). Pick the type of material, style, and color that express the real you, but don't go wild; you'll increase resale value by choosing a simple door style and a neutral color.

When selecting special cabinet accessories to customize your storage space, bear in mind that half your cabinets should contain no more than the standard shelving. Two favorite practical accessories: a lazy Susan or other rotating organizer to prevent items from disappearing into dark cabinet recesses, and a built-in metal bread box.

European-style cabinets use concealed, or cup, hinges, but variations are available to fit face-frame construction. These hinges are nice not only because you can't see them, but also because they let doors swing closed under their own steam when held an inch or two away from the cabinet.

Traditional face-frame cabinets have visible hinges. Many surfacemounted types such as strap, H, L, barrel, and knife styles look great on Early American-style cabinets. Note: Doors with these hinges may need catches to close.

TROUBLE • The edges of plastic-laminate doors and drawers are delicate. Look for cabinets that feature hardwood edges. They are less prone to breakage, and the wood adds ambience.

• If kids climb on a drawer, the drawer glides or guide rails may bend. But don't worry; replacing them is easy. Simply pull the drawer out and lift it gently to remove. Take it to a home center and find a matching glide.

Drawer glides, or guides, are the pieces of wood, plastic, or metal inside the cabinet that a drawer slides in and out on. The rail-like strips on the side of the drawer fit into the glides inside the cabinet.

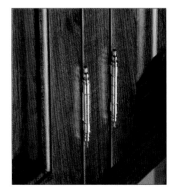

Once traditional hinges (above) are installed, the hinge can't be adjusted easily.

European, or cup, hinges (left) can be adjusted if the fit of the cabinet door gets loose or out of alignment.

CABINET MANUFACTURERS

Aristokraft 812-482-2527

Fieldstone Cabinetry 800-339-5369

Heritage Custom
Kitchens 717-354-4011

IXL Cabinets 800-527-5903

Kraftmaid Cabinetry 800-654-3008

Merillat Industries . . 800-575-8763

Omega Cabinets . . . 319-235-5700

Quality Cabinets . . . 800-298-7020

Starmark 800-594-9444

ISLANDS/EAT-INS

Want to add valuable square footage to counters and also partition kitchen space into dining, storage, and cooking centers? Then get an island. It can be either an extended counter called a peninsula counter or a stand-alone center island.

Thanks to improvements in plumbing and wiring, islands can be equipped with everything from sinks, cooktops, and dishwashers to under-counter TVs. If you're including a sink, talk to your plumber about the best way to vent it, since island sinks can't be vented in the same way that kitchen sinks are. Venting upward is also an issue when installing a cooktop—unless you select a downdraft unit, which vents downward.

In an open-design kitchen, a peninsula equipped with stools can be used to separate the kitchen from adjacent living areas without isolating the cook from surrounding activities.

Don't try to shoehorn an island into a small kitchen—the cramped quarters you'll create will cancel out any benefits offered by the island. Consider a built-in eating area instead. It will take up less room than a freestanding table, and almost any type of kitchen can accommodate one. Built-in banquettes and window seats let you squeeze in more people than conventional chairs do. Some other nifty ideas: you can tuck a small breakfast nook into the corner of an L-shaped space or make a snack bar out of one leg of a U-shaped kitchen.

If an eat-in kitchen's not your thing, substitute a desk or computer station to turn your kitchen into command central. To protect your computer from power surges, have an electrician install a dedicated circuit for it (see page 93).

Too many cooks spoiling the broth? Get an island. It not only adds extra counter and storage space, but also creates a socializing area that is separate from other work zones in the kitchen.

CRITICAL DIMENSIONS

 ✔ Leave at least 42" of clearance between an island and the cabinets opposite to allow the cabinet doors to swing freely. Leave 48" if you're installing a dishwasher or an oven in the island.

✔ For counter dining, allot an area measuring about 15" deep and 24" wide per person.

✔ Leave 36" between stools or chairs and the wall (or any furniture) behind them if people will be passing through; 24" is sufficient if there won't be any traffic. When measuring, position the seats where they will be when they are in use, not when they are parked under the counter.

 • No room (or no money) for an island in your kitchen? Put a stout farm or harvest table or a work cart on wheels in a convenient spot.

• For the easiest hit on your wallet, keep it simple. A cabinet composed of rectangular units is much more economical to install and much cheaper than designer configurations.

• If you can't exactly match the island to the countertop, go for something completely different. Choose from marble, butcher block, or ceramic tile.

• Live with an island or peninsula plan for a few days before making any final decisions. First, outline the addition with masking tape. Then count the number of times you step over the lines during the course of a normal day. Traffic problems will become obvious.

• If you're making the island out of stock cabinets, make sure to order them with finished sides, where they will be visible.

Eat-in islands are typically 10"–12" higher than the standard table and therefore require stools for seating. Get sturdy stools that have a staggered number of foot rests.

COUNTERTOPS

Plastic laminate is a popular choice for the countertop, especially when complemented with a ceramic tile backsplash (shown above). The bullnose (the edge of the counter) can also be decorative. Although Formica bullnose edging is the most common, ceramic tile, polished chrome, and narrow brass or hardwood are all worth considering. By building up layers of solid-surface material on the counter edge, you can even get multicolored pinstripes.

The workhorse of countertops? Plastic laminate, such as Formica. It's easy to clean, comes in numerous colors and patterns, and is the cheapest dollarwise. Alas, the surface can't be repaired easily. A ding in plastic laminate stays a ding forever.

Solid-surface materials, such as Corian and Avonite, are a step up. Depending on the manufacturer, they can be made from acrylic, polyester, or a combination of the two. Since the color goes all the way through, the look is richer–as is the price. Big advantage: the surface is repairable; a scratch in a solid-surface countertop will buff right out. An even bigger stride upward in quality is polished granite, but it's even more expensive. Although granite is durable, the light colors tend to stain and the dark colors will show scratches.

Other popular choices for countertops are hardwood butcher block (usually maple) and ceramic tile. The pluses? They're both durable and can give a kitchen warmth and personality. The minuses? Butcher block is not carefree; it gouges, burns, and stains easily, requiring spruce-up sanding. It also needs extensive hot-water washing to keep it germ-free. Ceramic tile has grout joints that must be cleaned and sealed annually to keep them sanitary and stain-free, but tile won't stain, gouge, or burn.

There are three parts to a countertop: the counter, the backsplash (the band at least 3"–4" high that protects the walls from spills and splashes), and the bullnose (the edge of the counter, usually made of matching counter material).

SHORTCUTS • Never cut raw poultry or meat on a butcher-block top or a countertop-inset made of wood; you risk bacterial contamination. Use a cutting board instead—it's easier to clean thoroughly before and after.

COUNTERSPACE SMART

You can never have too much counter space. Here are some rule-of-thumb minimums:

✔ Next to the sink: 18" on one side, 24" on the other.

✔ Next to the refrigerator: 36".

✔ On both sides of the oven: 15".

✔ On both sides of the cooktop: 12".

✔ Wood or tile makes a great island topper, or you can inset one where you need it in the countertops for chopping or holding hot pots. Unite these different materials by using the same edging as on the countertops.

✔ If the price of hand-painted tiles is prohibitive, use them for accent only. Mix a few decorative tiles into a field of neutral tiles for a little artistic splash.

Post-formed countertops are seamless, meaning that the countertop, bullnose, and backsplash are one solid piece. The advantage? No caulked seams to collect dirt or water.

COUNTERTOP MATH

PLASTIC LAMINATE: Prefabricated counters are the easiest to install. A professional can install a 2' x 8' section in about two hours. Pieced laminate takes an hour or two longer.

SOLID-SURFACE MATERIAL: This requires professional installation or you'll void the warranty. The fabricator will usually take measurements and create counter templates after the cabinets are installed. This will result in up to a week's delay before installation. Installation itself takes about six hours per 2' x 8' section.

GRANITE: Installation takes about six hours per 2' x 8' section. Use professional installers, because a 1¼"-thick countertop of this length can easily weigh 250 pounds, so there's a risk of breakage during installation.

CERAMIC TILE: It takes about five hours for a tile setter to lay a 2' x 8' section. Before tiling, a contractor will have to build a substrate (or base) made of either plywood or cement board.

COUNTERTOP MANUFACTURERS

Avonite, Inc. 800-428-6648

Dupont (Corian) . . . 800-426-7426

Formica Corp. 800-367-6422

Nevamar 800-638-4380

Wilsonart Int'l 800-433-3222

SINKS

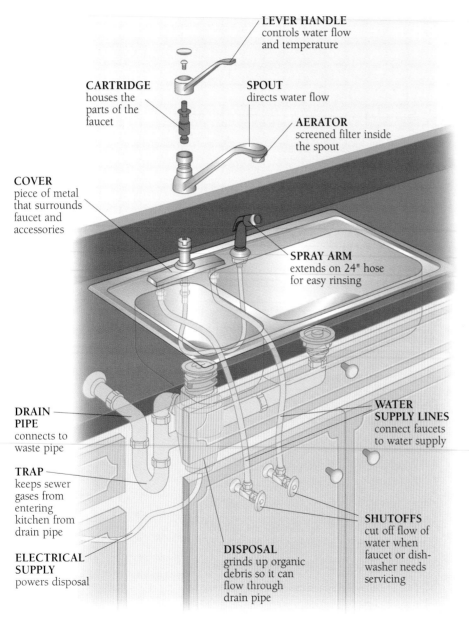

LEVER HANDLE
controls water flow
and temperature

CARTRIDGE
houses the
parts of the
faucet

SPOUT
directs water flow

AERATOR
screened filter inside
the spout

COVER
piece of metal
that surrounds
faucet and
accessories

SPRAY ARM
extends on 24" hose
for easy rinsing

**DRAIN
PIPE**
connects to
waste pipe

**WATER
SUPPLY LINES**
connect faucets
to water supply

TRAP
keeps sewer
gases from
entering
kitchen from
drain pipe

**ELECTRICAL
SUPPLY**
powers disposal

DISPOSAL
grinds up organic
debris so it can
flow through
drain pipe

SHUTOFFS
cut off flow of
water when
faucet or dish-
washer needs
servicing

Don't let accessories like built-in rinse baskets, colanders and drainboards drive your sink selection. Think about sink quantity, size, and material first. Do you want one, two or three sink basins? Whatever you decide, be sure to get at least one deep sink; you'll find it essential for washing large pots and platters.

Sinks can be made from stainless steel, enameled cast iron, or various composites (see page 100). A self-rimming sink is the easiest to install. It pops right into a hole in the countertop, with the sink's rim overlapping the counter. A surface-mounted sink has a separate stainless-steel edging that fastens the sink onto the countertop. An undermount sink has no rim or border so crumbs and messes on the counter can be sponged directly into it.

TIME FACTOR	
INSTALL	**PLUMBER'S TIME**
Sink	2 hrs
Faucet	2 hrs
REMOVE/REPLACE	**PLUMBER'S TIME**
Sink	3 hrs
Faucet	3 hrs

FAUCETS

Most kitchen faucets are single-levered. Why? Because they allow you to control both water flow and temperature with one hand. Faucets fall into two groups: those with washers and those that are washerless. Faucets with washers, called compression faucets, have two handles; single-handle faucets are usually washerless.

Nowadays faucets are more than a spout and handle. There are fun accessories to shop for and use. Do you want a sprayer, a built-in soap dispenser? Or how about a hot-water dispenser, which pumps out boiling water for tea and soup from its own hot-water heater under the sink? Sinks typically come pre-drilled with one to four faucet holes for accessories, but you can specify five. Make sure there are enough holes to accommodate all your accessories. If you change your mind later, you can always cover up the extra holes with buttons matching the color of your sink.

A gooseneck spout (left) or a long straight spout (above) is ideal for a kitchen sink because both designs allow large pots to fit underneath.

SHORTCUTS • Little leaks can cause big problems in the sink base cabinet below. Prevent them by occasionally, shining a light into those dark recesses, to make sure the faucet, sprayer, or other accessories aren't dripping.

• To prevent water seepage around the edge of the sink from damaging the counter, run a bead of silicone caulk along the joint between the sink and the countertop.

• For a quick, scratchless shine on chrome faucets, rub the metal with a little toothpaste on a damp rag.

TROUBLE • Clogged drain? Unplug a clog by vigorously pumping up and down with a plunger. To get better pressure, block the dishwasher drain by crimping the hose. Never use a liquid drain cleaner when plunging—it could splash back into your eyes.

• Irregular water flow? Check the aerator—the tiny screen in a faucet spout or sprayer that adds air bubbles to the flow of water. Unscrew the aerator from the spout. (Use pliers to loosen the sprayer nozzle to get to its aerator.) Turn on the water; if the flow is better without the aerator, it needs cleaning. Soak it in vinegar, then scrub it with a toothbrush.

SINK MANUFACTURERS

Eljer
Plumbingware 800-898-4048

Porcher 800-359-3261

Sterling Plumbing. . . 800-783-7546

FAUCET MANUFACTURERS

American Standard . 800-223-0068

Kohler 800-456-4537

DISHWASHERS/DISPOSALS

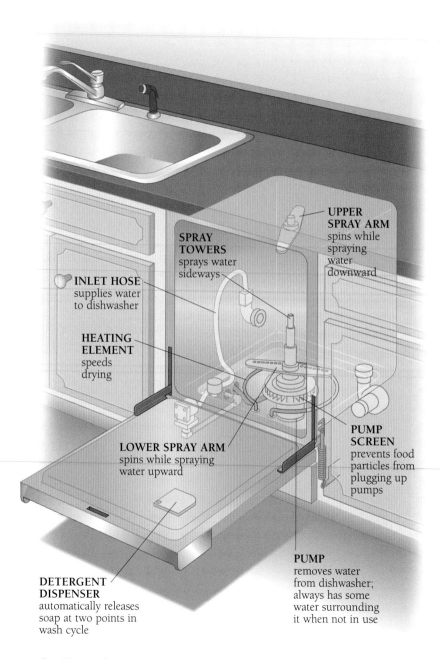

UPPER SPRAY ARM
spins while spraying water downward

SPRAY TOWERS
sprays water sideways

INLET HOSE
supplies water to dishwasher

HEATING ELEMENT
speeds drying

LOWER SPRAY ARM
spins while spraying water upward

PUMP SCREEN
prevents food particles from plugging up pumps

DETERGENT DISPENSER
automatically releases soap at two points in wash cycle

PUMP
removes water from dishwasher; always has some water surrounding it when not in use

Some things to consider: washing ability, capacity, noise, energy efficiency, and optional features. The basics? At least three wash cycles (many models offer seven), including a rinse-and-hold cycle, which allows you to rinse a partial load, then wait until the machine is fully loaded to complete the washing cycle.

The more expensive the machine, the more conveniences it will offer. One of the latest features is an electronic keypad that replaces push buttons and dials. Others include a childproof cycle-selection lock, an electronic cycle monitor, and a sensor that automatically adjusts the amount of hot water depending on whether the load is heavily or lightly soiled. If quiet operation is a priority, check out dishwashers with noise-reduction features.

Energy-efficiency models with internal temperature boosters provide the greatest savings. You can send 120°F water to the machine and the dishwasher will raise the temperature to the recommended 140°F. Smart tip: Before you start the dishwasher, run the hot water in the kitchen sink for a minute. This will prime the hot water coming into your dishwasher.

Dishwashers can be built-in or portable. Built-ins are adjustable in height (33¾"–35¼") so they can slide in under countertops. Portables, usually 36½" high, are separate units that can move around on their own rollers and are often topped with a wood or laminate work surface.

• Dishes not clean? Most problems result from one of two causes: 1) A clogged pump screen. Unscrew the spray tower, remove the arm and screen, poke out stuck particles in the screen with a toothpick. and rinse. 2) The water in the house is less than 140°F. Insulate the pipes that run between the dishwasher and the water heater, and/or raise the water-heater setting. (see page 139). Note: When there are children, elderly, or unsuspecting

guests in the house, higher temperatures can result in accidental scalding.

• Etched glassware? If you use too much detergent with soft water (or too little detergent with hard water), your glasses may become "etched" with a cloudy film. Adjust the amount of detergent you use. For hard water, get a water softener (see page 143).

Trash compactors are available as freestanding units or built-ins. They use "ram pressure" to compress trash to a fraction of its original size. Top-quality compactors feature rams with 5,000 pounds of pressure.

DISPOSALS

Before you buy a disposal, check with your local building department to find out whether they are allowed. If they are, ask what types are allowed. Most disposals are continuous-feed types—a flick of the switch and they're on. Batch-feed types have a built-in switch that activates the disposal only when you replace the drain stopper after loading the disposal. The more horsepower, the better. Budget models are usually equipped with a ½-hp motor; better models have ¾-hp; and top-of-the-line, 1-hp.

What shouldn't go down? In general, if it will rot, put it in. However, never put in bones. If the disposal gets a little smelly, deodorize it by throwing in a few lemon rinds.

TIME FACTOR

INSTALL	PLUMBER'S TIME
Dishwasher	1 hr
Disposal	1½ hr
(Plus 1 hour by an electrician, if not wired.)	
REPLACE	**PLUMBER'S TIME**
Dishwasher	2 hrs
Disposal	1 hr

DISHWASHER MANUFACTURERS

GE 800-626-2000

KitchenAid 800-422-1230

Maytag 800-688-9900

Miele 800-843-7231

Whirlpool 800-253-1301

DISPOSALS

In-Sink-Erator. 800-558-5700

Anaheim
Manufacturing 800-854-3229

LIGHTING

Fluorescent fixtures installed under cabinets and above sinks and stoves make excellent task lights. Before making a decision on the placement of an under-cabinet light, take a seat nearby and note whether you can see the fixture—you shouldn't be able to.

This is tricky. The kitchen is home to numerous activities—cooking, eating, paying bills, doing homework, you name it. To light these diverse tasks you may need to mix and match different types of lights that have various levels of intensity and focus. Ambient lighting is the most diffuse; it fills the entire kitchen with soft illumination (see page 28). Accent lighting is more focused; it highlights special objects and areas of the kitchen. Task lighting is usually the most focused; it is needed to brighten work surfaces without casting shadows.

Here's a roundup of various types of lighting fixtures and how to use them:

Ambient: Ceiling-mounted incandescent and fluorescent fixtures are typically used for ambient lighting. Fluorescent fixtures directed upward from atop cabinets will play off the ceiling to create easy ambient light that also gives a kitchen the illusion of more height.

Accent: Pendants, chandeliers, track lights, and recessed lights are popular choices for accent lights. You can use them with ambient lights when illuminating an eating area or snack bar. Your goal is lighting that enhances activities ranging from homework and paying bills to an informal dinner.

Task: Recessed lights, downlights, and pendants, when installed directly over workstations, serve as excellent task lights. Place them over the sink and stove and anywhere else you do work requiring clear illumination. To avoid casting your own shadow across a work surface, install task lights slightly in front of and above the surface.

Lighting the eating area can be tricky. Don't place in-ceiling recessed lights (the round circles in the ceiling, at left, also known as "cans") directly over a table. Pointed straight down, they can create sharp shadows, especially on faces. Try a pendant fixture with frosted shades like the one here. It takes bulbs of various wattages for soft or bright lighting effects, and the shades diffuse the light further. Or, if the shades are not frosted, lower the pendant to about three feet above the table.

SEEING THE LIGHT

CHECKLIST What color is your light?

✔ Incandescent light (the kind given off by standard lightbulbs) comes in a number of colors, from warm yellow to orange.

✔ Halogen gives off a bright white light. They burn hot—keep them away from anything combustible. (Consider using xenon lights instead; they give off less heat.)

✔ Fluorescent comes in many shades, but the most common is a bluish white. Full-spectrum light is available; its illumination is the closest to sunlight.

SHORTCUTS

• To make in-ceiling recessed lights do double duty as both task and accent lighting, install a dimmer switch. At 100 percent power, they function as task lights; at lower power, as accent lights.

• Light up your pantry with an automatic push-button light on the doorjamb. The light stays off until you open the door. Turning off the light is as easy as closing the door.

• Remember that light is absorbed by dark colors, so if your cabinets are dark, you'll need more light sources.

LIGHTING SOURCES

American
Fluorescent Corp. . . . 847-249-5970

American Lighting
Assoc. 214-698-9898

Cooper Lighting . . . 847-501-5455

Lightolier 800-223-0726

Juno Lighting 800-367-5866

Thomas Lighting . . . 800-365-4448

Underwriters
Laboratories 847-272-8800

REFRIGERATORS

A big decision, literally—both price-wise and sizewise. Refrigerators range in cost from several hundred dollars to well over $3,000, so determine your budget first. Size is next. Measure the width, depth, and height of your refrigerator area. Include enough clearance to open the door fully; otherwise, you won't be able to remove bins or shelves for cleaning.

Of all the refrigerator models out there, those with the freezer on top cost the least, are the most energy-efficient, and come in a slew of styles and sizes. Bottom-freezer fridges are pricier, but they let you comb through your fruits and vegetables without stooping. The big side-by-sides are more expensive and offer less usable space than top-freezer fridges of comparable size, but you can store part of your food at eye level in both the freezer and the refrigerator compartments.

Whatever your choice, insist on the basic features: easy-to-clean glass shelves (if they slide out, so much the better), see-through crispers, and a freezer light. Other niceties are automatic defrost, storage on one or more shelves for gallon-size containers, back-hung shelves (easier to raise and lower than those fixed at the sides), split shelves (for more flexibility in arrangement), pull-out freezer baskets, and a meat drawer with a separate temperature control to keep meat a few degrees cooler than other perishables.

Most appliance doors can accommodate decorative panels; however, some side-by-side refrigerators such as this one have weight restrictions for such panels.

SMART ORGANIZING

✔ Group "like with like"—snacks with snacks, drinks with drinks, and so on.

✔ Line the bins with paper towels to absorb moisture and expedite cleanup. Stow fresh fruits and vegetables in their own bins.

✔ Put little-used condiments on a plastic tray or lazy Susan at the back of the fridge; they'll be easier to find when needed.

✔ Store leftovers in clear containers toward the front of the refrigerator so you won't forget about them.

✔ Keep the freezer full for better efficiency. Throw in a loaf or two of bread to take up space if necessary.

✔ For the ultimate in organization, replace your old refrigerator with built-in refrigerated cabinets and drawers. These custom-built babies can be placed—almost invisibly—anywhere in the kitchen, so they will be located right where you need them, each one set at its own temperature.

ICE MAKERS

Many refrigerators come with built-in ice makers. If yours doesn't, you can buy a kit and have it installed. Either way, the plumber has to tap into a nearby water pipe and route the water through an inlet valve on the back of the fridge to the ice maker. When the ice supply runs low, this valve lets water in to create more ice. If the ice has an off taste, you may need to buy an in-line filter for the ice maker; it will remove chlorine and other unwanted minerals.

Refrigerators can be big-time energy hogs. Buy only as much refrigerator as you need. If you buy more, you'll pay for it twice—initially, and then again in each electric bill, since each cubic foot of space requires additional electricity. The average is 22 cubic feet (the amount in this bottom-freezer refrigerator) which is enough for a family of four. Shop for the most energy-efficient model you can find.

SHORTCUTS

• Increase energy efficiency by vacuuming your unit's condenser coils—which transfer heat from within the fridge to the outside—twice a year. The coils are either on the back or the bottom front, under the refrigerator door. If your fridge is an old model, replacing it with a new energy-efficient one of equal capacity will pay off; it can save you about $70 a year.

REFRIGERATOR MANUFACTURERS

Amana 800-843-0304

Frigidaire 800-451-7007

GE 800-626-2000

Jenn-Air 800-688-1100

Sub-Zero 800-222-7820

Whirlpool 800-253-1301

STOVES/MICROWAVES

Because they create combustion, stoves should be vented through a duct leading outdoors or by a recirculating vent inside. This microwave is designed to be installed over a stove, so it comes with a recirculating vent. It can also be connected to an outside vent.

Only two ways to go: either you get a stand-alone unit called a range which consists of a cooktop with an oven directly underneath, or you buy built-ins. A built-in cooktop (with or without an oven) is set into the counter. A separate oven can be inserted into a cabinet or wall anywhere you like. Because electric cooktops and ovens require a lot of energy, they must be hardwired on their own separate circuits. And because they generate so much heat they need to be vented.

The basic cooktop consists of four standard burners, but if you're willing to spend more you can incorporate a griddle, grill, rotisserie, or a fifth burner. Power for heating elements ranges from 1,200 to 2,600 watts for electric stoves, and from 9,000 to 12,000 BTUs for gas stoves. The higher the power, the faster the food will cook. Really serious cooks get commercial-style gas ranges powered with 15,000 BTUs. These big boys come with a backguard—a stainless steel plate that protects the wall behind the range from the stove's intense heat.

What's the difference between gas and electric cooktops? Speed and flexibility. An electric burner takes a while to heat and is controlled by a knob with a finite number of settings. Gas gives you instant heat and can be adjusted more precisely. For this reason, hard-core cooks usually opt for gas cooktops.

Now, about the oven. Electric ones use radiant heat from electric coils. Convection ovens also use radiant heat, but have a fan that circulates the air, so meats and poultry cook more evenly and brown 30 percent faster.

Newer electric cooktops, like the "smoothtop" (right), eliminate the need for a drip pan, which in conventional gas and electric (left) models is used to catch spills.

SHORTCUTS • A broiler may be located either in the upper part of the oven or below it. If possible, opt for the former; at waist height it's more convenient.

• The best cookware has flat bottoms that dispense heat evenly. Turn over the pot and stand a ruler on the bottom of it. If you see light between the edge of the ruler and the pot, the bottom isn't absolutely flat.

• Oven thermostats should be accurate to within 25°F when the heat in the oven is measured with an oven thermometer. If a thermometer shows that the temperature is off by more than 50°F, have the thermostat recalibrated. Call the manufacturer for instructions.

• If an electric oven isn't heating properly, simply replace the radiant heating element.

• To locate cold spots in your oven, bake a batch of cookies; the ones in the chilly areas of the oven will bake more slowly.

MICROWAVE OVENS

These clever appliances use fast-moving microwaves to heat the water in food. The convection/microwave combinations are the most versatile types, because they can employ either radiant heat or microwaves. Space-saving microwaves with built-in range hoods can be hung over stoves to provide a vent for the range as well as an extra cooking unit. Many free-standing microwave units are small, so they can be tucked away almost anyplace in the kitchen.

TIME FACTOR

INSTALL	INSTALLER'S TIME
Built-in Microwave	1 hr
Gas Range	45 min
Electric Range	30 min

NOTE: Time does not include installing electrical outlet.

STOVE/MICROWAVE MANUFACTURERS

Amana 800-843-0304

Frigidaire 800-451-7007

Garland 800-257-2643

GE 800-626-2000

Jenn Air 800-688-1100

Viking 888-845-4641

Whirlpool 800-253-1301

FLOORS/WALLS

Cooking involves a lot of standing, so be kind to your feet and get a floor covering that is springy. Wood and vinyl are easy on the feet, but ceramic tile and stone aren't. However, the springiness that makes floors pleasant to walk on also makes them more susceptible to dents and scratches than their harder counterparts. Vinyl tiles and sheeting are fairly easy to repair (see page 119), but dents and scratches in solid wood have to be sanded out (see page 29).

Watching your wallet? Stick with vinyl, but don't neglect quality. The best vinyl floor coverings are coated with a thick "wear layer" of between 25 and 35 mils (a mil is a thousandth of an inch), and their extra cost will repay you with many years of superior service.

Thanks to the current love affair with cabinets, even large kitchens have relatively little wall space. Whatever you do, make sure the kitchen walls you can see are covered with something durable and washable. If it's paint, go for gloss, semigloss, or eggshell. If it's a wall covering, choose vinyl; it can stand up to a good scrubbing.

For floors, textured surfaces and multicolored designs are better at concealing dirt than flat surfaces and solid colors. Go easy on the texture, though—larger peaks and valleys help to conceal dirt, but they can trap tiny pools of grimy water when they are mopped.

SHORTCUTS • Before vinyl can be installed, the subfloor must be absolutely clean and smooth. A speck of dirt or glob of paint on the subfloor will project through the face of vinyl flooring and look terrible.

• Ideally, border tiles should be at least half the width of the field tiles (see page 116). If the borders are skinnier, the proportions won't look right. Apply a border all around the room, not in one area only.

• Wood floors in kitchens may buckle if laid flush against the walls—they expand and contract more than usual due to the greater humidity changes caused by cooking. Leave an extra-wide expansion space of ½" between the floor and walls; where cabinets don't hide it, baseboards and moldings will.

• With both wood and vinyl floors, the best defense against damage is a good offense—place a doormat at each door to capture dirt and grit before it gets ground into the floor.

 CHECKLIST TYPES OF FLOORS

✔ Wood floors are available in solid or laminated strips, parquet, or planks. Wood may be prefinished or not.

✔ Vinyl tiles are typically available in 9" and 12" squares. Sheet vinyl is available in 5' or 12' wide rolls.

✔ Ceramic tile is available in squares, rectangles, hexagons, and octagons, as well as coordinating accent shapes of various sizes.

Ceramic tile is extremely durable, but alas very unforgiving to dropped china and tired feet.

Hardwood floors have country-style charm, but take more maintenance. Use mats in high-traffic areas.

FLOORING SOURCES

WOOD FLOORING

Bruce
Hardwood Floors . . 800-722-4647

Anderson
Hardwood Floors . . 864-833-6250

CERAMIC TILES

Daltile. 800-933-8453

Laufen Int'l. 800-758-8453

VINYL FLOORING

Armstrong 800-233-3823

Tarkett 800-367-8275

FAMILY ROOM

Home is where the hearth is. It's also where the books, stereo, TV, and VCR are. In short, it's the family's entertainment center.

FAMILY ROOM

To get family-room smart, use this easy number guide to identify and name all the parts of your entertainment hub.

FIREPLACE

1 . . . MANTEL

2 . . . GRATE

3 . . . ANDIRONS

4 . . . HEARTH

5 . . . DAMPER (not seen)

6 . . . SCREEN

7 . . . FIREPLACE TOOLS

BUILT-INS

8 . . . SHELVING

9 . . . BASE CABINET

WINDOWS

10 . . . FIXED WINDOW

11 . . . VERTICAL LOUVER
      SHADES

CEILING FAN

12 . . . CEILING FAN MOTOR

13 . . . BLADE

14 . . . DOWN ROD

LIGHTING

15 . . . TRACK LIGHTING
      (Accent lighting)

16 . . . READING LAMP
      (Task lighting)

FIREPLACES

Glassfront doors keep sparks from spilling onto the hearth, but they can get too hot to touch. Vents above and below this pre-fab fireplace circulate air to heat the room more efficiently.

A crackling wood fire in the fireplace makes a house seem more inviting. Whether you have a built-in masonry fireplace or a freestanding unit, it can be notoriously energy inefficient if it draws heated air from the house. (Remember, fire needs oxygen to burn.) The most efficient fireplaces draw in only outside air for combustion by means of air ducts that pull in fresh air from outdoors. (For information about the chimney, which is an extension of your fireplace, see page 128.)

Adding an energy-efficient fireplace will improve the comfort and value of your home. A popular new type of fireplace is called "zero-clearance." Essentially a metal cabinet attached to a metal chimney, it's called zero-clearance because it requires no bulky masonry casing to be fire-safe. It can be installed against a wall (traditional) or in the middle of a room (modern freestanding).

Nowadays many homeowners opt for gas-burning fireplaces, which are virtually maintenance free. The ceramic gas-fire logs are permanent and look almost like the real thing. Better still, gas does not give off harmful emissions when burned or leave a build-up of creosote. Note: Gas inserts are available for masonry fireplaces, but they require a metal flue liner. Whatever your choice, make sure your plans conform to local building codes and fire regulations.

WOOD BURNING SMART

CHECKLIST

✔ Logs burn more efficiently when air can circulate underneath them. Stack them on a raised grate or andirons.

✔ First make sure the damper is open. Then, before you light a fire, hold a burning torch of rolled-up newspaper near the damper for a moment to warm the cold air in the flue. This will create an updraft that will take the smoke away.

✔ Have the chimney cleaned annually by a licensed chimney sweep to get rid of dangerous creosote buildup (see page 129). *This oily brown substance is flammable and can cause chimney fires.*

Sculptural fireplaces like this are made of stucco with firebrick inside.

TIME FACTOR	
INSTALL	**MASON'S TIME**
Built-in masonry fireplace with chimney stack	**1 wk**
Gas insert and metal flue liner with piping to gas line	**2 days**
INSTALL	**CONTRACTOR'S TIME**
Zero-clearance gas or wood-burning fireplace	**2 days**
Wood-burning stove with piping to vent	**2 days**

WOODSTOVES

Here's the secret of the popularity of woodstoves: they burn wood more slowly and evenly than fireplaces do, so less heat escapes through the chimney. Wood-burning stoves are generally made of steel or cast iron. They can be vented through an existing flue, (which means you can place them in a fireplace) or through their own freestanding chimney (generally made of metal tubing that winds its way up through the roof or the side of the house). Stoves with a thermostat activated damper control that automatically adjusts airflow to keep the fire alive can burn unattended for up to eight hours. Woodstoves are rated by the Environmental Protection Agency (EPA) for emissions. *Safety note: The entire exterior of a wood-burning stove and its freestanding flue can get very hot. That's good for radiating heat; just don't touch it.*

FIREPLACE MANUFACTURERS

Heat-N-Glo 800-669-4328

Heatilator 800-843-2848

Majestic Products . . 800-525-1898

Superior Fireplace . . 800-854-0257

WOOD-BURNING STOVE RESOURCES

Jotul USA 207-797-5912

Rais & Wittus 914-764-5679

Travis Ind. 206-827-9505

SHELVES

Built-in shelves add a classic—as well as highly useful—element to a home that adds to its resale value. Try to match the shelves' finish and molding to the rest of the room.

Got a lot of arty things you want to show off, or do you need space to store belongings neatly? Either way, put up shelves. They do tend to dominate a room, so if it's display you want, place them at the room's focal point. If it's storage that is needed, then install shelves in hallways, within an alcove, or under windows.

Custom-made built-in shelves give a room a finished look and can be designed to meet present and future needs. Points to discuss with the carpenter are 1) size of the objects to be displayed or stored (for example, electronic equipment, large-format books, or sculpture), and 2) electrical outlets needed for equipment or lighting.

Your built-in choices are simple: 1) fixed shelves in a case with a "face frame" (plain strips of wood or molding overlapping the case's edges) or 2) ready-made adjustable shelves that are anchored to the wall by metal or wooden standards. (The standards have slits in them for attaching metal or wooden brackets to support the shelves. Standards, shelves, and brackets are available in various lengths and widths at most home centers.)

Think carefully about the type of shelving material you want. Hardwood is beautiful, but it is the most expensive type of shelving. Plywood veneered with cherry, oak, or birch is a good choice, but its edges are rough; cap them with strips of wood, or for a fancier look, use molding (see page 34). Pine is inexpensive and lightweight, but it sags under heavy loads. Avoid pressboard, as it can sag excessively.

SHORTCUTS

• For the look of custom-made built-in units at a fraction of the cost, check out unpainted-furniture stores. The dealer is often willing to build a unit to your specifications. Once the bookcase is in place, complete the look by having a carpenter add molding (page 36) to the edges.

• If shelves are more than 24" wide, install a center support standard to keep the shelf from sagging.

• Tame shelf clutter—small toys, tools, and gadgets—with boxes and decorative wicker baskets. For easy identification of opaque boxes, label them on the outside with tape or metal-ringed price labels sold at most stationery stores. See-through plastic boxes with lids are terrific for kids' stuff.

• For dramatic—yet inexpensive—display lighting, attach a row of small spotlights or reading lamps along the top molding of a bookcase. Plug the lights into a multi-plug outlet hidden on the top shelf and run the wire down the back of the shelves to the nearest wall outlet.

• When arranging shelves, place heavy objects at waist height to prevent back strain when putting them away. Reserve top shelves for display or for infrequently used, fairly lightweight objects.

Rear-mounted shelves should be anchored to the studs (the wooden structural supports behind the wall).

TIME FACTOR

INSTALL	CARPENTER'S TIME
Built-in shelves	3 days
Ready-made shelves	1 hr

NOTE: For six shelves (6" wide x 1" deep)

SHELVING MANUFACTURERS

Knape & Vogt 800-253-1561

Ply Gem
Manufacturing 800-752-1478

S & S Wood
Specialties 800-242-9663

Spur—USA 513-985-1000

SKYLIGHT

Like skylights, roof windows (shown here) allow natural light to fill the room. Both can be stationary or operable to allow for ventilation.

A skylight will turn a gloomy family room, bathroom, or hallway into an airy space. There are two types—fixed and ventilating. Fixed skylights don't open; they usually consist simply of a double pane of glass or plastic. Ventilating skylights open like an awning window to let in air. If the ceiling is low enough for you to reach, the skylights are called roof windows. If the ceiling is high, get a motorized opening mechanism that you can operate from below instead of using a telescopic pole.

When buying a skylight, there are a couple of points to bear in mind: glare and heat loss or gain. What you want to look for is a skylight that has a high R-value (the rating of the material's ability to resist the transfer of heat). The higher the R-value, the better.

To cut down on harsh direct sunlight, place the skylight on the north side of the roof. If you can't do that, consider buying skylights that have shade screens. Better yet, buy low-E glass, which significantly lowers glare and heat radiation. It has a high R-value.

Installing a new skylight is not a spur of the moment improvement. You'll need to check your local code requirements, and you'll probably need a building permit. Putting in a skylight means a carpenter has to 1) open up a section of the roof; 2) frame the skylight opening; 3) build a shaft through the attic connecting the roof to the room's ceiling; 4) install the skylight; and 5) patch the roof around the skylight.

CEILING FANS

Ceiling fans are nifty climate controllers. How so? Because they have switches you use for changing the direction of the blade rotation to either pull up or push down the air in the room. A ceiling fan can be used to pull warm air up above the living area when the weather is hot and push it down when it's chilly. Buy the best fan you can afford; the expensive ones operate more efficiently, quietly, and reliably than the cheaper brands.

Many ceiling fans come with light fixtures attached. Be careful: Some fixtures attached at a downward angle can throw an unpleasant glare onto walls or shine directly in the eyes of those sitting below it. Instead, look for a light fixture that diffuses the light evenly in the space around it. Note: Light bulbs can become loose from the vibration of the fan, solve the problem by purchasing shakeproof ceiling-fan light bulbs.

Ceiling fans are heavy. For safety's sake have the electrician mount the ceiling fan to a ceiling joist. (Joists are the support beams in a ceiling and floor). To prevent ceiling fan vibration and noise, get a model with a dropped motor, if your ceiling height allows.

The longer the down rod, the better the fan can circulate the air in a room.

TIME FACTOR	
INSTALL	**CARPENTER'S TIME**
Skylight	2 days
INSTALL	**ELECTRICIAN'S TIME**
Ceiling fan	1–2 hrs

Blades should have a 12° pitch to help air flow.

SKYLIGHT MANUFACTURERS

Andersen Windows 800-426-4261

Velux-America 800-888-3589

CEILING FAN MANUFACTURERS

Concord Fans 800-677-7326

Hunter Fan Co. 800-448-6837

HOME SAFETY

Smoke detector and tester

Carbon monoxide detector

Fire extinguisher

 THINGS TO BUY ✔Smoke detectors: One on the ceiling of every level in the house—as well as in the basement and garage—is the minimum requirement. (New construction codes require that smoke detectors be wired directly to household wiring so they are battery-free.) Place detectors in central areas, such as the hallway, but away from bathrooms or kitchens, where steam or cooking smoke will trigger them. If the house has attached extensions (workshops, mudrooms, and so on), install detectors in those areas, too. Ideally, each bedroom should have its own detector. Test detectors monthly to make sure batteries or wiring is working. Change batteries annually. Pick a memorable day, such as a birthday or holiday, when you will change the batteries.

✔Carbon monoxide detector: Mount one near the furnace. It can sense the presence of carbon monoxide, a poisonous, odorless gas that may be given off by faulty heating devices.

✔Fire extinguishers: They are essential safety devices. You should be able to reach one from the kitchen. Place others near potential fire hazards such as fireplaces and stoves. Fire extinguishers are marked with large capital letters: A is for fires involving wood and paper; B for flammable liquids, such as grease or paint; and C for electrical fires. For general use, get ABC extinguishers, covering all types of fires. Extinguishers only handle small fires; get out of the house and call the fire department if flames are not quickly contained.

✔Fire blankets: Keep one in the kitchen and others near the fireplace and workshop to smother all kinds of fires, even chemical fires.

✔Rubber nonslip mats: Put the mats under your area rugs to make them skidproof.

✔Safety glass: Windows close to the floor (18" or lower) should have safety or tempered glass—which is shatter-resistant.

✔Decals: Sliding glass doors should be marked with small decorative decals, placed at the eye levels of both children and adults.

✔Exterior lighting: Install enough lights to allow safe navigation of walks, steps, and entrances.

STUFF TO DO ✔Emergency medical kit: Create your own and keep it handy in the pantry or family room (never in a moist area like a bathroom). It should contain bandages, antibiotic ointment for cuts or stings, syrup of ipecac (in case of poisoning), and tweezers.

✔Emergency phone numbers: Make a list of key phone numbers—those of relatives, family physicians, and the local hospital, plus the poison control center, insurance policy numbers, etc. Keep the list near the phone.

✔Fire escape routes: Plan escape routes for each room of the house. Check which windows can be climbed out of safely. If there are no safe escapes from upstairs bedrooms, purchase a rope ladder and store it in the master bedroom.

✔Paints and toxic materials: Store paints, flammable liquids, and spray-paint cans in closed containers well away from any source of ignition, such as a furnace, heating duct, or water heater. Note: These products must be disposed of properly.

✔Electrical wires and TV cable: Electrical cords and cable cords—especially those near entryways—should be taped to the baseboard so they won't be tripped over.

CHILDPROOFING

THINGS TO BUY

✔ Professional child-proofers suggest that grown-ups get down on all fours and roam the house, especially the family room and the kitchen. Look for dangerous items at or near eye level: outlet sockets, radiators, heating vents, windowsills, edges of tables and chairs, and so on.

✔ Window locks and latches: Fit windows with locks and safety latches, which allow them to be opened slightly for ventilation, but not enough to crawl through. Just be sure they can be completely unlocked and opened in case of emergency.

✔ Toilet latches: Lock down toilet lids with plastic latches.

✔ Window guards should be installed on any unlocked windows above the first floor.

✔ Outlet plugs: All outlets not in use should be plugged with rubber plugs so children can't stick anything into the sockets.

✔ Stove shields: Protect little hands from hot burners with stove shields.

✔ Rubber rims/Fabric shields: Sharp corners on tables, rockers, chair backs, or pointy spindles should be capped with rubber rims that can be glued on. Corners and rough edges on fireplaces or large coffee tables can be wrapped with elastic fabric shields.

✔ Safety latches: Use on cabinets or drawers that are off-limits to children. It's especially important to latch kitchen and bathroom cabinets and drawers. Keep sharp knives and other dangerous objects out of reach.

✔ Shatter-resistant glass: Replace glass in shower doors, French doors, and coffee tables with safety laminated glass, or cover it with a special clear plastic film you can get at hardware stores. If the glass should break, this film will contain the shattered pieces. Remove anything near glass doors or windows that a child can climb on or trip over.

✔ Safety gates: Block off the tops and bottoms of stairs and any other unsafe areas with sturdy safety gates.

✔ Heating devices: Cover radiators. Block off fireplaces and space heaters with screens.

✔ Beds/Furniture: Crib slats should be no more than 2⅜" apart. Keep window shade pulls away from cribs. Climbable furniture such as bookcases should be bolted to the floor or wall.

✔ Stair and deck balustrades: They should be spaced so that a sphere 4" in diameter cannot pass through. If it can, cover the balustrades with a plastic guard or safety net.

STUFF TO DO

✔ Cleaning supplies, flammable items, and medicines (including vitamins and other supplements): These should be removed from low cabinets and shelves and placed out of the reach of children.

✔ Check chips of peeling paint in older homes for lead content with a lead-testing kit. If the content is dangerously high, have the paint removed or sealed professionally.

✔ Emergency phone/info list for baby-sitters: Include the name and birth date of each child; note any allergies or medical conditions; list phone numbers of relatives, neighbors, doctors, and a poison control center.

✔ CPR: Take a course on infant-and-child CPR offered at most community centers.

✔ Hot water temperature: Check your hot-water heater. To avoid scalding, it should be set no higher than 120° (see page 138).

Outlet plug

Window guard

SAFETY SOURCES

Lowe's Home
Safety Council 800-723-3466

National Safety
Council 800-621-7619

One Step Ahead
(catalog) 800-950-5120

Perfectly Safe 800-837-5437
(catalog)

GET HOUSE SMART

BEDROOMS

This is your refuge, your dream palace, your fun station. Read on to learn how to make it as private, soundproof, and attractive as you can.

BEDROOMS

This easy number guide will help you identify and name the parts of your bedroom. Read the following pages for complete explanations.

WINDOWS

1 . . . DOUBLE-GLAZED CASEMENT WINDOW

2 . . . CASING

3 . . . CRANK (not shown)

4 . . . BALLOON WINDOW TREATMENT

WALLS/CEILINGS

5 . . . CROWN MOLDING

6 . . . WALLPAPER BORDER

7 . . . FLAT PAINT

8 . . . SEMIGLOSS PAINT

FLOORS

9 . . . WALL-TO-WALL CARPETING

10 . . . BASEBOARD

11 . . . HEATING REGISTER

LIGHTING

12 . . . LAMP (Task Lighting)

INTERIOR DOORS

Doors are either right- or left-handed, depending on the placement of the hinges.

A standard interior door measures 6'8" high and 24"–36" wide. The door of choice? A solid-core door with recessed panels.

Are you replacing an old door or installing one where no door has gone before? The distinction is important because doors are sold in two configurations: door-only and pre-hung. If you buy the former, you get just the door, which is all you need for a replacement. A prehung door comes attached to its accompanying frame, called a jamb, and holes have been bored for the doorknob and strike (the receptacle that the latch slides into). The prehung type is what you will want for a new door installation.

Interior doors do not have to be as sturdy as exterior doors, which battle the elements, but they do have to be substantial enough to block out unwanted sound, light, and visitors. There are three basic types of doors to choose from: solid wood, solid core, and hollow core. The differences boil down to the usual battle between quality and price.

Solid doors are just that—solid wood—and consequently, they are the longest-lasting. Solid-core doors are generally made of particle-board between two layers of wood veneer. Both solid and solid-core doors reduce sound transmission nicely. They are ideal for bedrooms and baths. Hollow-core doors are made of honeycombed cardboard that is covered with a layer of wood veneer. They don't wear all that well, nor are they great at soundproofing—use them for closets. Smart tip: Make an inexpensive door look expensive by covering it with compressed fiberboard facing that also helps it resist warping and swelling.

SHORTCUTS

• Make a small room bigger with a "pocket door," a sliding door that fits into a pocket in the wall. (A standard swing door can cut into a room's space). To make the wall pocket, a carpenter creates a hollow opening in the wall next to the doorway. The door slides inside the wall on tracks leading into the pocket.

• Older houses have narrow doors. Gain valuable inches by installing swing hinges, which allow a door to open past the hinge. Ideal for wheelchair users, who need a 34"-wide door passage.

TROUBLE

• Door out of line? Tighten all the screws in the hinges. If it's still out of whack, check if the problem is at the top of the door or the bottom. If top, then replace the middle screw in the top hinge with a 3" screw. (If bottom, then deal with the bottom hinge.) The longer screw will help hold the door in line. If that doesn't do it, the door must be removed and its edges planed down to better fit the doorjamb. Call the carpenter.

• Swinging doors? Get a doorstop.

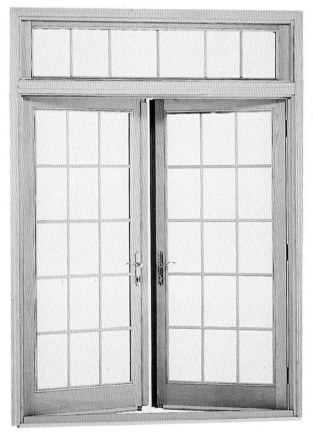

A prehung door like this double French door is already hung in its frame, so there's no bother with hanging it on hinges. French doors can be used as an exterior and interior doors.

DOORKNOBS AND LOCKS

A doorknob with a button lock, called a privacy lock, is good for a bathroom or bedroom door because it will lock from the inside. In case of emergency, this lock can be opened by inserting a pin or screwdriver into the hole on the outside knob. There is also the key-in-knob lock, which has both an inside button lock and an outside key lock.

DOOR MANUFACTURERS

Bend Door Co.	800-346-5252
Caradco	800-238-1866
Masonite Corp. (CraftMaster)	800-405-2233
Morgan Mfg	800-766-1992
Premdor	800-663-3667
Simpson Door Co.	800-952-4057
Sun-Dor-Co	316-284-0044

WINDOWS

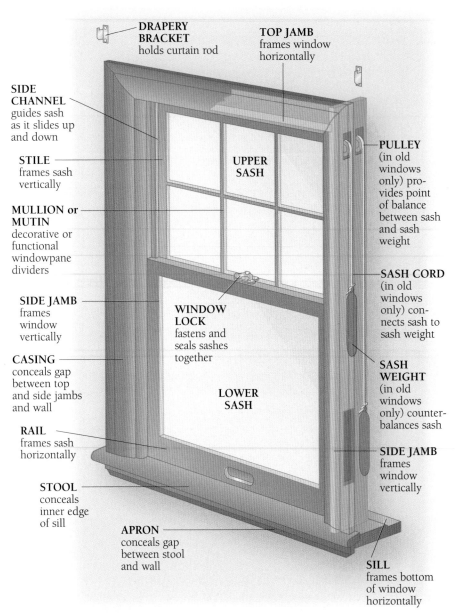

DRAPERY BRACKET
holds curtain rod

TOP JAMB
frames window horizontally

SIDE CHANNEL
guides sash as it slides up and down

STILE
frames sash vertically

MULLION or MUTIN
decorative or functional windowpane dividers

SIDE JAMB
frames window vertically

CASING
conceals gap between top and side jambs and wall

RAIL
frames sash horizontally

STOOL
conceals inner edge of sill

APRON
conceals gap between stool and wall

UPPER SASH

WINDOW LOCK
fastens and seals sashes together

LOWER SASH

PULLEY
(in old windows only) provides point of balance between sash and sash weight

SASH CORD
(in old windows only) connects sash to sash weight

SASH WEIGHT
(in old windows only) counterbalances sash

SIDE JAMB
frames window vertically

SILL
frames bottom of window horizontally

This is pretty straightforward: windows come in two basic types: ones that open, called operable, and ones that don't, called fixed. The most common operable type is the double-hung window, in which both upper and lower window sashes slide open vertically on tracks. Other window types include casement (hinges on the sides, sash opens outward like a door), awning (hinges on top, sash tilts outward), hopper (hinges on the bottom, sash tilts inward), and sliding (sashes slide sideways).

When it comes to choosing glass, however, it gets a little overwhelming. Here is a roundup of the types available: *Sheet glass* is found in older homes. *Tempered glass* will break into tiny beads, not long shards, when broken. *Safety glass* has a thin layer of film between two layers of glass, which keeps fragments of glass from flying when broken. *Obscure glass* is frosted glass. *Low-E glass* has a thin coating of metal oxides that blocks out certain types of solar rays. An *insulated window* has two panes of glass separated by a vacuum, and is called double-glazed. The space between the panes is what insulates the window from heat loss. A *gas insulating window* has argon or krypton gas between the panes for better insulation. (See page 154 for info on screens.)

TIME FACTOR	
WINDOW INSTALLER'S TIME	
Remove and replace window	2-3 hrs
Repair sash	1 hr

WINDOW TREATMENTS

✔ Before you buy, consider the effect you want to create, the view outside, and how much privacy you want and/or need. The following treatments can be bought in various standard sizes or be custom-made.

✔ Blinds (either vertical or horizontal) give a clean look and are great for controlling the amount of light a room receives, particularly where the sun is very strong (the south and west sides of a house, for instance).

✔ Roller shades made from fabric or vinyl are good for room darkening. For better energy efficiency, get roll-down shades that have metallized fabric backing to reduce drafts as well as light.

✔ Drapes or curtains, especially lined ones, cut drafts, control light, and act as a barrier to sounds from the outside world. If the light (or the view) is harsh, add a layer of sheer fabric or lace to soften it.

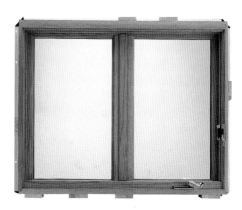

Casement windows are attached by hinges to only one side of the window frame and open outward by either cranking or pushing a lever.

 • For inexpensive energy efficiency, get window film. It is see-through plastic that adheres to windows. It saves on heat loss in winter and cuts down on fading of upholstery and drapery fabrics in summer. Get low-E film for maximum efficiency.

• Cut down on outside noise as well as drafts by installing interior acrylic storm windows. They attach to the inside of windows with Velcro or magnetic strips.

• If you want to replace a large window, check out commercial window manufacturers who make display windows for stores. These windows are often less costly than special orders for residential windows.

 • Window won't open? It was probably painted shut. Break the paint seal by slicing it carefully with a utility knife or a single-edged razor between the window and the frame.

• Double-hung windows hard to open? Rub a bar of soap along both of the window's tracks or spray them with a lubricant.

• Drafty windows? In many homes, heat lost through cracks around windows accounts for about 20 percent of the heating bill. Apply weatherstripping (foam-rubber strips with adhesive backing) along the rails at the top and bottom of each window.

• Fog inside your insulated window? It's vacuum seal is broken, replace the window.

Want to open up a room that already has an operable window? Add a fixed window, like the half-moon one shown above.

WINDOW MANUFACTURERS

Andersen Windows. 800-426-4261

Hurd Millwork 800-433-4873

Marvin Windows . . . 800-346-5128

Pella 800-847-3552

Pozzi Window Co. . 800-821-1016

Peachtree 888-888-3814

Weather Shield 800-477-6808

WALLCOVERINGS

Wallpaper going partway up the wall can mimic wainscoting. A dense floral border along the ceiling appears to lower it, giving a cozy, sheltering look to the room.

Wait! Before you even think about choosing a pattern, consider what the room will be used for. Vinyl wallpaper is sturdier than paper wallpaper, so it can be scrubbed clean, making it ideal for kids' rooms, bathrooms, kitchens, and hallways. Paper and foil wallcoverings are a bit more delicate than vinyl; use them for the master bedroom and formal rooms.

Most wallpaper is sold as double rolls—roughly 56 sq. ft., which will cover an 8' x 7' portion of a wall. More will be needed if patterns have to be matched. Always buy at least one roll more than you think you'll need. For easier installation, select wallcoverings that are available "prepasted," which means that the backing is already coated with glue. Just wet it and affix to the wall.

Okay, now you can begin the agony of choosing the pattern. Some smart decorator advice: Bold overall patterns and large stripes can make a large room seem more cozy and intimate but will dominate a small room. An airy, delicate pattern will open up a small room and is generally more restful to the eye. If the walls are not straight—especially in old houses that might have settled—avoid patterns with strong horizontal motifs which will emphasize the unevenness along ceilings and floors.

PREPARE THE WALLS

CHECKLIST ✔ Old wallpaper should be scraped off and the walls scrubbed clean of any remnants of glue.

✔ All holes and nicks in the wall should be patched, especially if you are hanging a mylar or metallic paper.

✔ The walls should be primed with sizing or a good sealer. This will make repositioning during application easier and speed removal when redecorating.

TROUBLE • Tears in the wallpaper? To repair tears, use wallpaper seam sealer to glue edges back together. (Don't use household glue.) Wallpaper seam sealer is available at most hardware stores. For large, ragged tears, first remove the damaged area of wallpaper, then cut a new piece of wallpaper to exactly match the size that was removed; carefully seal in the new piece.

SHORTCUTS • For a finished look, detach switch plates and outlet plates, cover them with wallpaper, and reattach them.

• Wallpaper borders are a fast way to change the look of a room. Simply glue the border directly over the existing wallpaper or painted walls. Besides the traditional placement at the top of the wall, try running the border midway along the wall for a chair-rail effect.

• The first strip of wallpaper usually should be hung in an inconspicuous place (behind a door, for example) so that any mismatches between the first and the last strip won't be noticed as much.

Big bold patterns will overwhelm small rooms; use them for big rooms. Smaller patterns are best for small rooms. First timers, keep it simple and choose random patterns; they are a lot easier to deal with than ones that need to be matched.

Borders are all the rage. Why? Because without putting in much effort, they can instantly transform a room. Use them to complement a painted wall or wallcovering, or hang them in place of ceiling trim—especially the embossed patterns.

TIME FACTOR

	PAPERHANGER'S TIME
Prime walls	1 ½ hrs
Wallpaper walls	3 hrs
NOTE: Estimate is for a 12' x 12' room	

WALLCOVERING SOURCES

F. Schumacher
(Waverly, Village) . . . 800-552-9255

Imperial
Wallcoverings 800-222-3700

Sherwin-Williams. . . 800-474-3794

Sunworthy 800-523-8006

York Wallcoverings . 800-375-9675

CARPETING

Plush carpeting like that shown above is so soft, your feet feel like they're melting; high-quality plush won't even show your footprints.

Yes, it's expensive, but wall-to-wall carpeting muffles noise, hides flaws in the floor, and is more energy-efficient than hardwood floors. A room's use should help determine the type of carpeting you need. For example, kids' rooms, family rooms, and stairs get heavy-duty use, so cover them with hardwearing carpet that has tightly twisted, cut-pile. Living and dining rooms receive less wear and tear and warrant a plusher-pile carpet. Save the velvets and deep, feathery piles that are so soft on bare feet for master and guest bedrooms, which typically get light use.

How can you tell how well a carpet will wear? Good question. To answer it, the Carpet and Rug Institute has developed a performance rating system that ranks carpet on its ability to stand up to heavy traffic. A carpet is ranked from 1 to 5. The higher the rank, the heavier the traffic the carpet can handle and still retain its appearance. Good news: These rankings are noted on the back of most carpet samples. Now for some carpet savvy—the heavier the face weight of the carpet, the tighter the stitching, and the more times the fiber is twisted, the better the carpet's quality.

SHORTCUTS

• Smudges found on carpets near entranceways usually come from the dirt outside, so consider the color of your local soil. If it's light or sandy, buy carpeting of a lighter color; buy reds, greens, blues, or browns for areas where the soil is dark.

• To make a room look larger and grander, consider edging your carpet with a made-to-order carpet border.

• Install mildew-resistant carpeting in rooms that are prone to water condensation (bathroom, laundry room, basement).

TROUBLE

• Allergies? Allergy-sensitive people may be troubled by the various chemicals that new carpeting and padding release into the air. Most of the chemicals will evaporate in the first 48 to 72 hours after installation. Stay away until then.

TIME FACTOR

INSTALL	CARPET LAYER'S TIME
Wall-to-wall carpeting with padding (small room—12' x 12')	2 hrs
Wall-to-wall carpeting with padding (large room—20' x 20')	3 hrs

Loop pile—surface formed by yarn loops of uniform length.

Hard Twist—cut pile that has been twisted, then set.

Cut Pile—top of loops trimmed for a smooth, soft surface.

Berber Loop Pile—blends of different shades of yarn.

Sisal Style—a ropelike texture.

PADDING

Invest in the best padding you can afford. The good stuff can be pricey, but it will greatly extend the life of the carpet as well as add cushioning and insulation to the floor. For wall-to-wall carpet, you need a pad that is at least ½" thick. There are three basic types of padding: rubberized felt, sponge rubber, and urethane foam. Felt resists tearing, but it can mildew if it gets soaked (it's not good for humid climates). Sponge rubber and foam may tear, but they won't mildew.

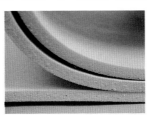

CARPET MANUFACTURERS

Beaulieu United 800-227-7211
(Coronet)

Daltonian 800-788-1408

Mohawk Carpets . . . 800-241-4494
(Aladdin, Karastan)

Shaw 800-441-7429
(Philadelphia)

World Carpet 800-241-4900

Wools of
New Zealand 800-367-0462

CLOSETS

The ultimate luxury? A customized built-in closet that fits all your wardrobe and storage needs.

Here's the trick to making your closet work for you: organize it by what you wear most often. Everyday clothes, including shoes, belts, ties, and bags, should be the easiest to reach. Next, group these items by quantity and size. In other words, see how many short items, such as shirts, folded pants, and jackets, versus the number of longer garments, such as dresses and robes, you have.

If the closet is deep and high, create two sections. Put two rods in one sec-tion (the lower rod 40" above the floor and the upper rod 80" above the floor) for holding two tiers of short garments, such as shirts and folded pants. In the other section put the rod approximate-ly 60" above the floor for longer items. Ready-made closet organizers with rods and shelving are available at home cen-ters and can be adapted to fit various closet sizes.

To accommodate standard hangers comfortably, a closet needs to be at least 24" deep. Shelves can start 2" to 3" above the rods and go as high as 24" from the ceiling. They can also run along the sides and on the floor below hanging clothes.

Once you've organized your everyday clothes, consider storing the rest of your wardrobe—formal wear, seasonal garments, sports gear, and so on—in a separate area. If you can't, place them in a large garment bag and hang it at the far end of your closet.

 CHOOSING
CLOSET DOORS

Many closets typically have openings larger than the standard 36"-wide interior door. Here are some options:

✔ Bifold doors have pins on the top and bottom of the doors and are hung on a single upper track. The doors fold together like the bellows of an accordion.

✔ Sliding doors have top rollers and bottom guides, but are hung on separate tracks so one door can glide past the other.

✔ For greater ventilation, choose louvered doors (the slats allow more air to circulate). Mirrored doors are another option, but be careful of loading the door tracks with too much weight.

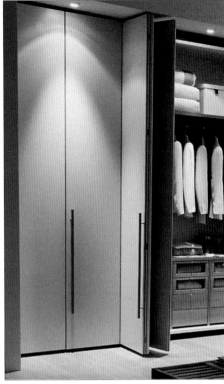

Bi-fold doors (like the one shown here) allow for greater viewing of your clothes than sliding doors.

 • Too dark? Don't overlook closet lighting. Have an electrician install an overhead light that goes on automatically when the door is opened. In a pinch, simple battery-operated lights that attach to closet walls are available at most home centers.

• Sliding door dragging? Look behind the door on the roller for a screw or an adjustment nut. Loosen it, adjust the door slightly higher or lower, and tighten it again.

• Sliding door stuck? Check the track for dents. Small dents can be evened out by squeezing them with pliers. Large dents can be smoothed by placing a block of wood behind them and hammering them flat.

• Moths? Don't carpet the closet—moths will use it for breeding; keep the closet floor clean. Encase clothes in airtight bags. In sealed storage closets, place strips or balls of naphthalene (mothballs) or camphor high up in the closet, as vapors travel downward.

CLOSET MANUFACTURERS

California Closets . . 800-873-4264

Closet Factory 800-692-5673

Cubbies Unlimited . . 800-282-2437

Custom Closet Co. . 800-360-1314

Poliform 212-421-1220

KIDS' ROOMS

Teenagers' rooms are awash in electronic equipment. To prevent overloading, add extra outlets (see page 93). Also, be sure to use surge protectors to help guard that expensive equipment from occasional power surges.

Most grown-ups forget this, but as children grow, so do their furniture needs. First, the bed. Children are in cribs until they outgrow them, usually when they are two to three years old, or 39" tall. (Note: The slats on older cribs may be spaced too far apart so that a little head could get stuck between them. They should be no more than 2⅜" apart.) When they are ready for a bed, get one that is low to the ground, to soften likely spills. The options are a child's bed, a grown-up bed with bed guards, or a mattress on the floor. Children are ready for grown-up beds around the age of five. (See page 75 for childproofing.)

Next, the desk. The most important consideration is the desk's height. It should be no more than 28" high. Because the desk will also be used as a drawing board, a play area, and a storage bin, make sure it's strong. For easier cleaning, the desk should have a laminated surface or, if wood, be varnished instead of painted.

The desk chair should be very stable and fit the child, allowing the feet to touch the floor. Take your child and have him or her try out the chair before you buy. Avoid swivel chairs to minimize the danger of toppling over.

All shelves and bookcases in a child's room should be securely bolted to the walls. Of course, your darlings won't climb on them, but a playmate might.

LIGHTING

CHECKLIST ✔ Children under the age of 13 should have small, unbreakable lamps in their rooms. Make sure to use a bulb with low voltage—or a fluorescent light—to avoid burns if the bulb is touched.

✔ Teenagers need desk and bed lamps that will take high-wattage lightbulbs; they are better for reading. Fluorescent lights are easier on the eyes, but teenagers may appreciate (and therefore use) the snazzy designs of the newer halogen desk lamps. Note: Halogen bulbs get extremely hot and can cause a fire if knocked over. (See page 28 for lighting.)

✔ Plug-in night-lights are a great way to light the path to the bathroom. Choose ones that are light-sensitive; they automatically come on when it's dark.

KIDS' ROOM MATH

Be prepared to redo their rooms at least four times while they are still a tax deduction. Babies need cribs and changing tables; little kids need beds and chest of drawers. Grade school kids need desks and play space. Teenagers need storage for their way cool stuff.

Bunk beds are fun and great space savers if the room is being shared, or if sleepovers are part of your kid's social scene.

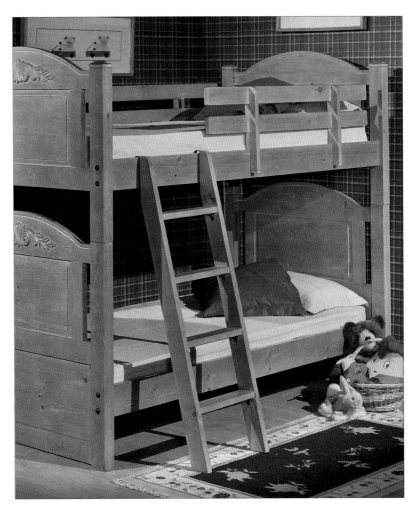

KIDS' FURNITURE SOURCES

Broyhill 800-327-6944

Ethan Allen. 203-743-8000

IKEA 610-834-0180

Lexington Furniture . 800-539-4636

Skools, Inc. 800-545-4474

HOME OFFICE

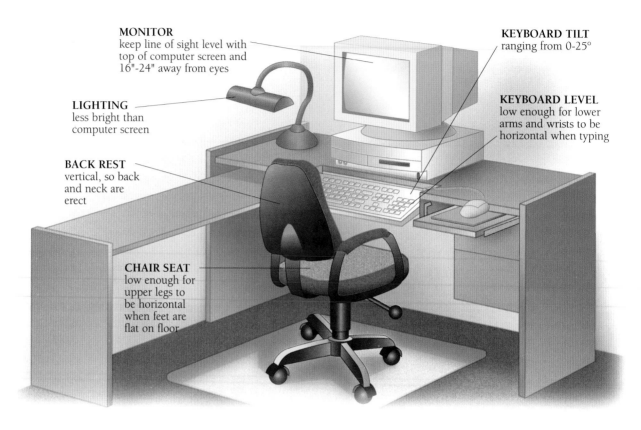

MONITOR
keep line of sight level with top of computer screen and 16"-24" away from eyes

LIGHTING
less bright than computer screen

BACK REST
vertical, so back and neck are erect

CHAIR SEAT
low enough for upper legs to be horizontal when feet are flat on floor

KEYBOARD TILT
ranging from 0-25°

KEYBOARD LEVEL
low enough for lower arms and wrists to be horizontal when typing

The computer keyboard usually should be lower than the regular desk height, so that when you type, your elbows will be bent at right angles. The chair should be low enough so that when you sit, your knees are bent at right angles.

Oh, the joy of working in your pj's. A home office can be tucked into any unused corner of the house, but the ideal location is a spare bedroom, especially if it's slightly removed from the general household hustle and bustle.

Any desk will do, provided it's the right height. If you use a computer, consider a computer desk. The keyboard rests on a panel that is lower than the regular desk to allow for comfortable typing. It is joined to other surfaces where you can spread out your papers.

Invest in an ergonomically designed chair. The back and seat of this type of chair are shaped to give maximum support to the spine while minimizing stress on the sciatic nerve. Your feet should be flat on the floor, and the chair should force you to sit up straight, with your spine against its back.

Storage systems do not have to be limited to filing cabinets—you can use baskets, kitchen-style cabinets, or bookshelves. Industrial metal shelving, painted the same color as the walls, is a good choice for cheap, sturdy shelves.

TROUBLE • Computer screen eye-strain? Cut down on glare from a bright office light by using a three-way bulb. Put it on low when you operate the computer. Move the monitor so that it doesn't reflect sunlight.

• Surges in electricity? These are caused by lightning, brown-outs or appliance overload and can damage computers and phone lines. Get a surge protector or suppressor at an office-supply-store and plug all electronic equipment into it. Shop for a special surge protector designed to plug the phone into; it can save both phone and modem.

• Need another line for a fax or an extra phone? Call the phone company to have a phone line installed.

EXTRA OUTLETS

A home office needs at least the same amount of electricity as the kitchen—20 amps. Most bedrooms have a 15-amp circuit. If you need more juice for extra electronic gear, call in an electrician (see page 17 about hiring one). An electrician can add a new "dedicated" circuit without ripping up the walls by using a "raceway" system. This system is made up of ½" to 8" wide plastic or metallic channels that are surface mounted to the wall or ceiling. These raceways conceal the new wiring while providing a surface for outlets and switches. Note: A dedicated circuit has its own electrical line and its own fuse or circuit breaker to better protect whatever is plugged into it from power surges, (see page 140 for more info).

If you can't convert a room into a home office, then get a computer wall unit like the one above and place it in the family room. Just pull up a chair and you're in business.

HOME OFFICE RESOURCES

I t's a retreat, a beauty salon, a home health spa. Most important, it's your last stop before you greet the world each morning. So take extra care and do this room right.

BATHROOM

TIME FACTOR

RENOVATE	TIME
Small bathroom	2–4 wks
Large bathroom	4–12 wks

NOTE: Renovation may require a plumber, electrician, tile setter, carpenter, and painter.

BATHROOM

To get bathroom smart, use this easy number guide to identify and name all the parts of your bathroom. Detailed explanations of each item follow in this chapter.

SINK

1 . . . BASIN

2 . . . PEDESTAL BASE

3 . . . DRAIN (not shown)

4 . . . DRAIN PIPE

5 . . . FAUCET HANDLE

6 . . . SPOUT

7 . . . OVERFLOW DRAIN

8 . . . WATER SHUTOFF

ACCESSORIES

9 . . . MOUNTING FLANGE

10 . . . GLASS SHELF

LIGHTING/ ELECTRICAL

11 . . . WALL FIXTURE

12 . . . MIRRORED INSET CABINET

13 . . . HEAT LAMP/VENT (not shown)

14 . . . GFCI OUTLET (not shown)

BATHTUB

15 . . . SHOWERHEAD

16 . . . SINGLE-HANDLED TUB and SHOWER FAUCET

17 . . . TUB SPOUT

18 . . . CAULK (around tub)

TOILET

19 . . . TANK

20 . . . TANK LID

21 . . . BOWL

22 . . . FLUSH HANDLE

23 . . . ANCHOR BOLT

24 . . . WATER SHUTOFF

BIDET

25 . . . HOT and COLD WATER HANDLES

26 . . . WATER SHUTOFF (not shown)

TILE

27 . . . FIELD TILE

28 . . . ACCENT TILE

29 . . . BULLNOSE TILE

30 . . . GROUT

WALLS/FLOORS

31 . . . DECORATIVE TRIM

32 . . . BASEBOARD MOLDING

33 . . . HARDWOOD FLOORING

34 . . . FLOOR TILE

35 . . . VINYL WALLPAPER

36 . . . HIGH-GLOSS PAINT

PLANNING

MINIMUM "FULL BATH" CLEARANCES

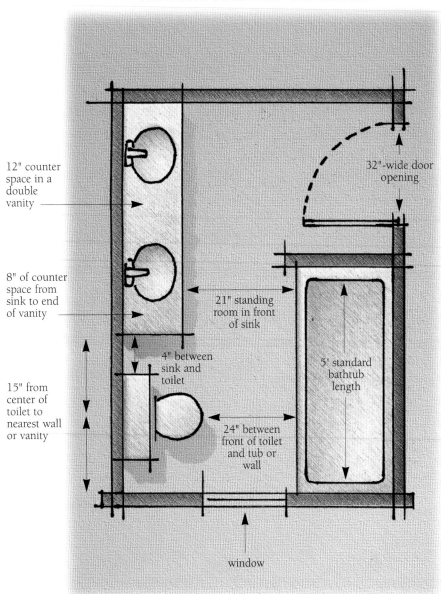

12" counter space in a double vanity

8" of counter space from sink to end of vanity

15" from center of toilet to nearest wall or vanity

21" standing room in front of sink

4" between sink and toilet

24" between front of toilet and tub or wall

5' standard bathtub length

32"-wide door opening

window

Nothing adds to your personal happiness like a well-designed bathroom. A smart bathroom not only is comfortable and attractive but also anticipates your family's needs well into the future. To that end, many bathroom designers are guided by a concept called "universal design," which makes bathrooms user-friendly to a broad range of people, including young children, the elderly, and the disabled, not to mention, primping teenagers. So whether you're renovating, starting from scratch, or simply want to make a few changes, keep this thought in mind: easy and safe access for everyone.

CHECKLIST

BATHROOM DO'S AND DON'TS

✔ Make the bathroom as big as you can. Grab extra space from an adjoining room, if you need to. Linen and bedroom closets are often built near bathrooms. Break down the wall and appropriate the space.

✔ Every fixture (toilet, sink, tub) must have a waste line, a plumbing vent, one or two water-supply lines, and shutoff valves. The size and composition of the pipes for these lines is determined by building codes. Moving plumbing fixtures even a few inches one way or another adds to the complexity and cost of the job. Why? Because the plumbing has to move with the fixture.

✔ In cold regions, don't install supply pipes in exterior walls, or they may freeze.

✔ Fixture colors vary from manufacturer to manufacturer, and even basic beige won't always match. Try to buy all your new fixtures from the same source at the same time.

✔Look over your new fixtures carefully before they are installed. If your new sink, toilet, tub, or faucet is defective, the manufacturer's warranty will pay for a reorder, but not for the labor involved in taking out the problem one and putting in a new one.

✔Electrical outlets in the bathroom must be of the GFCI type (see page 140). The GFCI protects against possible shock caused by an electrical device (like a hair dryer) coming into contact with water.

✔Every bathroom needs suitable ventilation, either by an operable window or by a fan or vent connected to the outdoors.

✔Good lighting is key. You want light over the shower or tub area and light by the sink and the mirror.

✔Create as much storage space as you can. Get the biggest medicine cabinet the bathroom can accommodate. And don't forget to make room for the laundry hamper.

✔When re-doing a bathroom in an older or historic home, use fixtures and tile that match the time period.

✔Make the bathroom wheelchair-friendly. The door needs to be at least 32" wide when open. To get more door space, put swing-clear hinges on the door. Have clear floor space for each fixture–a minimum of 30" x 48". The top of the sink should be no higher than 34". Anchor grab bars into wall beside tub, toilet, and shower. Install single-lever faucets and a handheld showerhead. Put a fold-up bench in the shower or tub. See page 19 for more ideas.

MINIMUM "HALF BATH" CLEARANCES

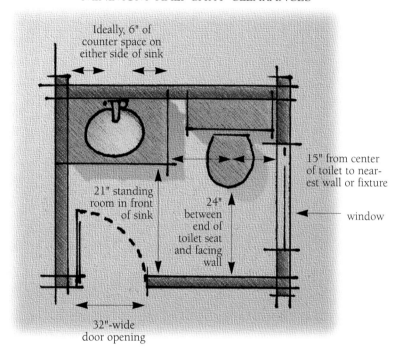

Ideally, 6" of counter space on either side of sink

15" from center of toilet to nearest wall or fixture

window

21" standing room in front of sink

24" between end of toilet seat and facing wall

32"-wide door opening

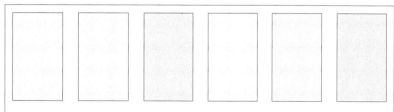

POPULAR FIXTURE COLORS

Why are most sinks, toilets, and tubs white? Because white doesn't show water spots, it's easier to find white replacement parts later, and it won't offend prospective home buyers. Although it's clearly the smart choice, white can be boring. Other light colors can be just as appealing, here's a sampling.

SINKS

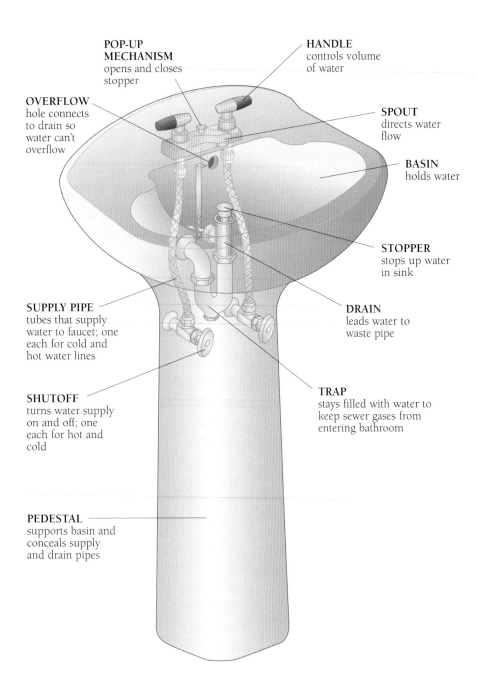

POP-UP MECHANISM
opens and closes
stopper

HANDLE
controls volume
of water

OVERFLOW
hole connects
to drain so
water can't
overflow

SPOUT
directs water
flow

BASIN
holds water

STOPPER
stops up water
in sink

SUPPLY PIPE
tubes that supply
water to faucet; one
each for cold and
hot water lines

DRAIN
leads water to
waste pipe

SHUTOFF
turns water supply
on and off; one
each for hot and
cold

TRAP
stays filled with water to
keep sewer gases from
entering bathroom

PEDESTAL
supports basin and
conceals supply
and drain pipes

This is easy. There are basically two types: a sink that fits on a pedestal base and a sink that sits inside a vanity (also known as a cabinet). A pedestal sink makes a small bathroom feel bigger, but it won't store much more than a toothbrush. That's why it's the sink of choice for the powder room. A vanity fills out big bathrooms and gets points for storage. However, it is usually more expensive.

Vanity sinks can be separate from the countertop or an integral part of it. The latter makes for easier cleaning, but if something goes wrong with the sink or the countertop, the whole thing may have to be replaced. If the sink is separate from the vanity, you have three style choices: self-rimming, rimless, or undermount. For all three, a matching-size hole is cut into the countertop, which could be wood or a solid man-made material, such as Formica or Swanstone. (If wood, the countertop needs to be covered with tile or marble.) Once the countertop is covered, the sink is slipped in and secured to the countertop.

Most sinks—whether vanity or pedestal—come in two types of material: 1) cast iron with porcelain enamel and 2) steel with porcelain enamel. Cast iron is heavier and more expensive than steel, but it lasts longer. Beware the inexpensive fiberglass sink, it's noisy and requires special cleansers.

CHOOSING A SINK

✔ Find out how much countertop you need by making an inventory of your toiletries. Each item typically takes up 2" square.

✔ Pedestal sinks offer little counterspace. Remedy this by adding a shelf or cabinet above the backsplash. Vanity sinks have more counter space. (Ideally, you want at least 8" to 12" on either side.)

✔ Before buying a pedestal sink, check with a plumber. Your new sink must match the height of your water-shutoff/supply pipes. (If you want a tall pedestal sink, the water shut-off pipes can be raised, but it will cost extra.) A vanity sink can be any height because it doesn't need to align with supply pipes.

SHORTCUTS • Bathroom vanity cabinets can be pricey. Save money and buy a chest that will accommodate a bathroom sink.

• In a really tiny bathroom, use a wall-hung or corner sink. This type of sink attaches directly to the wall (special mounting blocks in the wall are required). Pipes will be visible.

TROUBLE • Green stains on the sink or tile grout? You may have "hard" water. Have your water tested. Try special cleansers that work on stains caused by iron and lime.

• Clogged sink? Lift out the sink stopper and fish out the clog with a bent coat hanger or force it down with a plunger. Avoid chemical drain cleaners—they're hard on pipes.

Self-rimming sinks like this one sit on the countertop.

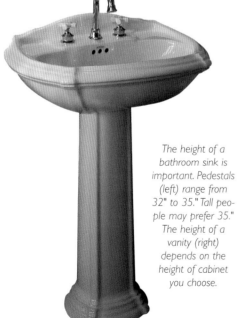

The height of a bathroom sink is important. Pedestals (left) range from 32" to 35." Tall people may prefer 35." The height of a vanity (right) depends on the height of cabinet you choose.

TIME FACTOR

REPLACE	PLUMBER'S TIME
Vanity sink	3 hrs
Pedestal sink	2 hrs
MOVE	**PLUMBER'S TIME**
Sink (vanity or pedestal)	3–6 hrs

NOTE: Plumber may have to move water-supply lines, the drainpipe, and plumbing vents.

SINK MANUFACTURERS

American
Standard 800-223-0068

Eljer 800-898-4048

Kohler 800-456-4537

Sterling Plumbing . . 800-783-7546

St. Thomas
Creations 800-536-2284

SINK FAUCETS

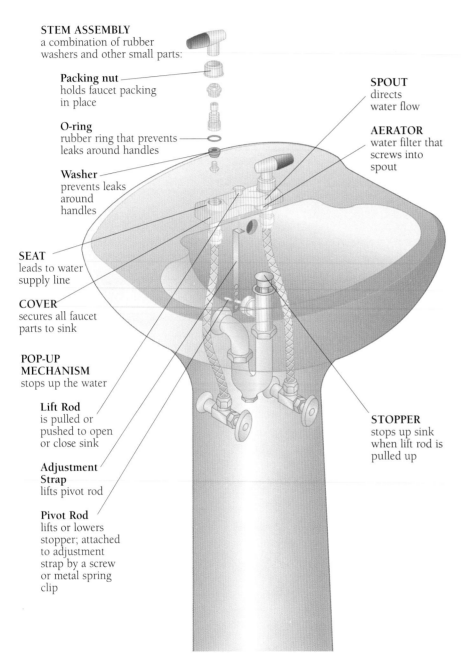

STEM ASSEMBLY
a combination of rubber washers and other small parts:

Packing nut
holds faucet packing in place

O-ring
rubber ring that prevents leaks around handles

Washer
prevents leaks around handles

SEAT
leads to water supply line

COVER
secures all faucet parts to sink

POP-UP MECHANISM
stops up the water

Lift Rod
is pulled or pushed to open or close sink

Adjustment Strap
lifts pivot rod

Pivot Rod
lifts or lowers stopper; attached to adjustment strap by a screw or metal spring clip

SPOUT
directs water flow

AERATOR
water filter that screws into spout

STOPPER
stops up sink when lift rod is pulled up

Get ready for sticker shock: faucets can cost as much as the sink. The best faucets have brass bodies and will last indefinitely; lesser-quality faucets are mostly steel. The insides of the faucets come in various configurations, such as *cartridge* (the parts are housed in a metal sheath) and *compression* (the parts are held together with a stem screw). Cartridge is usually more expensive than compression. Cheaply made faucets will corrode faster than those made with better materials. Quality always pays off in the long run, so bite the bullet and put down your money.

All faucets can be divided into two basic categories: two-handle models, which control water flow and temperature with separate knobs, and mixing models, which employ a single handle. There are a number of handle shapes to choose from: octagon, metal loop, lever, cross, and wrist blade.

Once you've decided on a handle type, choose a spout: standard, swivel, or gooseneck. Now choose the material: chrome silver, gold plate, or colored enamel. Finally, pick a finish: matte or polished. All done.

TIME FACTOR

REPLACE	PLUMBER'S TIME
Faucet washers or cartridge	1 hr
INSTALL	**PLUMBER'S TIME**
New faucet	1 hr

BUYING NEW FAUCETS

✔ The distance between bathroom sink handles is 4" or 8" (or 12" for kitchen faucets). Each sink is drilled with holes to match these standard spacings. Your new faucet must match your previous faucet's spacing.

✔ All the faucets and drains in your bathroom should have the same color finish. Cool colors call for chrome; warm colors go well with gold plate or brass.

• Uneven water flow? The aerator is clogged. Unscrew it and rinse out the debris, then screw it back into the faucet.

• Leaky faucet or spout? If you are handy, try fixing it yourself. If it's a compression-type faucet, the washer and O-ring may be worn out. Bring them to your local hardware store and get replacements. If it's a cartridge-type faucet, the entire cartridge has to be replaced, bring the whole cartridge stem to your local hardware store. If leaking persists after these fixes, the seat may need to be replaced. That calls for a special tool—borrow it or call the plumber.

• Loose stopper? The metal clip (or sometimes it's a screw) that holds the pivot rod in place may have come off. Look for it inside the vanity or on the floor and reattach it.

For a large sink, consider faucets that are not fastened to a body (above). This allows you to spread out the faucet handles to the maximum 8".

Lever handles are a popular design because they are easy to use, requiring little hand strength.

Four-inch faucets (above) are great space savers— a smart choice for small sinks. A single-handled mixing model (right) takes even less room.

FAUCET MANUFACTURERS

American Standard	800-223-0068
Delta Faucet	800-345-3358
GROHE	630-582-7711
Moen	800-289-6636
Peerless Faucet	800-438-6673
Sterling Plumbing	800-783-7546
St. Thomas Creations	800-536-2284

TOILETS

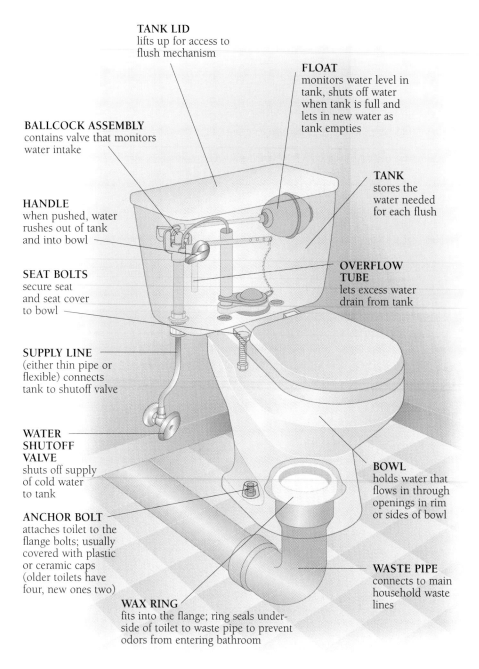

TANK LID
lifts up for access to
flush mechanism

FLOAT
monitors water level in
tank, shuts off water
when tank is full and
lets in new water as
tank empties

BALLCOCK ASSEMBLY
contains valve that monitors
water intake

TANK
stores the
water needed
for each flush

HANDLE
when pushed, water
rushes out of tank
and into bowl

SEAT BOLTS
secure seat
and seat cover
to bowl

**OVERFLOW
TUBE**
lets excess water
drain from tank

SUPPLY LINE
(either thin pipe or
flexible) connects
tank to shutoff valve

**WATER
SHUTOFF
VALVE**
shuts off supply
of cold water
to tank

BOWL
holds water that
flows in through
openings in rim
or sides of bowl

ANCHOR BOLT
attaches toilet to the
flange bolts; usually
covered with plastic
or ceramic caps
(older toilets have
four, new ones two)

WASTE PIPE
connects to main
household waste
lines

WAX RING
fits into the flange; ring seals under-
side of toilet to waste pipe to prevent
odors from entering bathroom

All toilets are made of vitreous china. What is vitreous china, you ask? It's fired clay with a glazed coating. This coating makes the china more sanitary because the coating is impervious to water.

Toilets come in two basic configurations: two-piece (the bowl and the tank are separate parts connected by two bolts and a rubber gasket) and one-piece (the bowl and the tank are a single unit). One-piece toilets are usually more expensive and quieter than two-piece toilets. Both can have either a round or an elongated seat.

Owing to increasing concern about water conservation, toilet codes are changing. Old-time standard toilets use about 6 gallons of water with every flush. Since the typical family flushes 16 times a day, that's a lot of water lost. Newer water-saving toilets use 3.5 gallons. The latest model is the 1.6-gallon toilet; in fact, in some parts of the country, it may be the only toilet you can buy. (Note: You don't have to replace an existing toilet with a water-saver unless you're remodeling and your local building code specifies the 1.6-gallon model. But less water used means more money saved in water bills, and a happier Earth.)

TIME FACTOR	
REPLACE	**PLUMBER'S TIME**
Toilet	3 hrs
Flushing mechanism	½ hr

One-piece toilets (above) sit lower to the floor, which makes them visually less obtrusive than two-piece toilets (right). Jazz up either with a toilet seat of contrasting color. The seat on the right is contoured with molded hand grips—great for the kids.

BIDETS

A bidet resembles a toilet, but it has hot and cold running water for bathing your private parts. It's easy to use—simply straddle it, turn on the water, and wash. If a bidet is important to you, find a line of toilets that includes bidets so the colors match. Remember to budget for installation of new water lines, waste pipes, and vents for the bidet. And don't forget to install a soap holder and a towel rack within reach.

CHECKLIST

BEFORE YOU REPLACE A TOILET

✔ Check the dimensions of the old one first: measure from the anchor bolt to the backwall. It will be either 12" or 14"—these are called rough-in dimensions. The flange (a metal collar screwed to the subfloor) can accept different anchor-bolt configurations.

✔ Colored toilets cost about 25 percent more than white; elongated bowls are more expensive than round; and the toilet seat is usually not included in the cost of the toilet.

TROUBLE

• Clogged toilet? Get out the plunger. If that doesn't work, call the plumber who will remove the toilet and "snake" the waste pipe with a long metal hose called a closet auger. Skip chemical cleansers—they're hard on pipes and awful for septic systems.

• Toilet continually overflows for no reason? The flushing mechanism inside the tank needs to be repaired or replaced. The parts aren't expensive, but the job usually calls for a half hour of labor.

TOILET MANUFACTURERS

American Standard . 800-223-0068

Kohler 800-456-4537

Eljer Plumbingware . 800-898-4048

Porcher 800-359-3261

Sterling Plumbing . . 800-783-7546

BATHTUBS

Unless your idea of a tub is nothing more than a glorified shower base, go for maximum soaking space. The average standard is 5' long and 32" wide; however, longer as well as wider tubs are available for extra bucks. Among your options are 1) the traditional claw-footed freestanding tub, 2) the one-sided tub that fits snugly between three walls, 3) the tub surround, which combines tub and surround wall, and 4) the drop-in tub, which fits into a wooden frame built for it by a carpenter. (The top of the frame is then covered with tile, fiberglass, or another waterproof material.) Most whirlpools and Jacuzzis are drop-ins because the frame conceals the requisite piping, wiring, and pump motor.

Tubs are made of various materials. The best and most expensive models are made of thick enameled cast iron, which is quieter and keeps water hot longer than other materials, such as enameled steel. However, they are extremely heavy, especially when filled with water; have an engineer check to make sure your floor joists can handle the weight. Acrylic and fiberglass tubs are lighter and mid-priced. Newer composite tubs are made of a thick plastic layer bonded to the back of enameled steel. These tubs are half the weight of cast-iron tubs and less prone to chipping. They hold heat nicely, too.

This is the standard one-sided tub with a separately tiled wall. Caulk (sealant) is used to seal the edge of the bathtub to the tile and floor. Grout goes between tiles to hold them in place.

BEFORE BUYING A NEW TUB

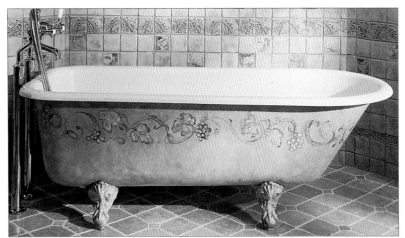

With most bathtubs, the water pipes are usually hidden in the wall. This is not so with the old-fashioned freestanding tubs (above).

✔If you're replacing an existing tub, measure it and make sure the new tub will fit and that the plumbing and tub drain are in the same place; drains are referred to as "right" or "left" drains.

✔Both a tub surround and a whirlpool are big. Make sure the tub will fit the stairway and the bathroom door.

✔Buy any other new fixtures (toilets, sinks) at the same time to ensure a color match.

✔Decide whether you want shower curtains or sliding glass or plastic doors. If you convert to sliding doors, you can go back, just know that removing the doors' side-rails will leave small holes in the walls.

Whirlpool baths (above) have four or more jets. The pump must be wired and grounded and have an access panel for easy servicing.

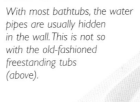

The standard one-sided tub (left) is 5' long, but 6' models are available—however, they're more costly and may require a special order.

TROUBLE • Cracks in caulk? Caulk is the waterproofing sealant used where the tub meets the tile. Unlike grout, it expands and contracts. Clean out the entire damaged area and reapply fresh caulk, available in tubes at hardware stores.

• Floor rot? Look closely at where the floor meets the tub. Any damaged subfloor should be repaired before you install a new tub.

TIME FACTOR

INSTALL	PLUMBER'S TIME
Cast-iron tub	6 hrs
Fiberglass tub	5 hrs
Fiberglass surround tub	7 hrs
Whirlpool (add 1 hour for an electrician)	8 hrs

BATHTUB MANUFACTURERS

American Standard . 800-223-0068

Aqua Glass 800-632-0911

ASB (Trayco) 800-355-2721

Jacuzzi 800-678-6889

Kohler 800-456-4537

Waterworks 800-927-2120

TUB FAUCETS

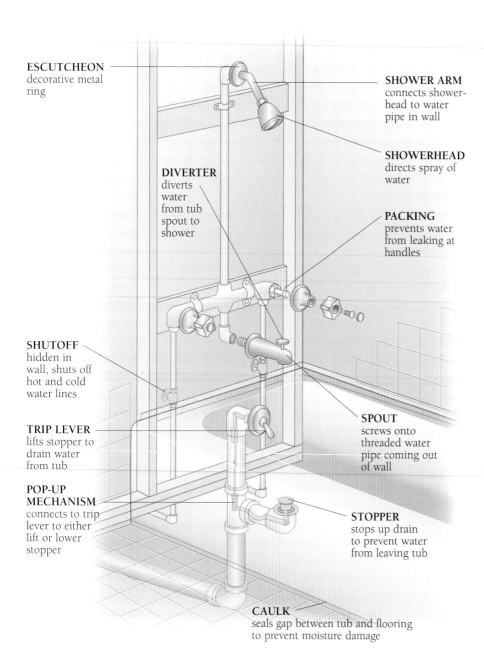

ESCUTCHEON
decorative metal
ring

DIVERTER
diverts
water
from tub
spout to
shower

SHUTOFF
hidden in
wall, shuts off
hot and cold
water lines

TRIP LEVER
lifts stopper to
drain water
from tub

**POP-UP
MECHANISM**
connects to trip
lever to either
lift or lower
stopper

SHOWER ARM
connects shower-
head to water
pipe in wall

SHOWERHEAD
directs spray of
water

PACKING
prevents water
from leaking at
handles

SPOUT
screws onto
threaded water
pipe coming out
of wall

STOPPER
stops up drain
to prevent water
from leaving tub

CAULK
seals gap between tub and flooring
to prevent moisture damage

Most newer tubs and overhead showers share the same water-supply lines, and so use the same faucet. A little lever in the tub spout called a diverter directs the water to either the showerhead or the tub spout.

As with sink faucets, you can choose a single- or double-handled faucet. *What's important is getting a tub faucet that is pressure-balanced.* Why? Because you don't want to be scalded or have the water flow stop because someone in the house flushed a toilet or turned on the dishwasher while you were in the shower or tub. This is a problem in older homes or homes with well water. Only single-handled tub and shower faucets have this pressure-balance feature.

HANDHELD SHOWER

If you bathe more than shower, consider getting a detachable hand-held shower. It is ideal for shampoo-ing and rinsing hair and makes cleaning the tub or whirlpool a snap. It can be mount-ed at either the showerhead or the tub spout. You may prefer a hose made of a materi-al that does not conduct heat.

ACCESSORIES

One easy way to spiff up the bathroom is to buy new toilet paper holders, towel racks, soap holders, toothpaste holders, and grab bars. They can be made of metal, plastic, wood, or ceramic. Toilet paper holders should be positioned slightly in front of the bowl and 26" above the bathroom floor. Position towel racks where you need them: by the sink and near the tub or shower. Place soap holders on the tub wall, about 12" up from the top of the tub. If the tub doubles as a shower, consider installing an additional soap holder at elbow height.

A grab bar should be placed on the tub wall directly above the top edge of the tub. One should also be on the wall closest to the toilet. Don't use a small towel bar as a grab bar; it is not designed to support your weight. All grab bars must be anchored on studs. Ideally, all your bathroom accessories should be anchored on studs.

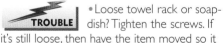

TROUBLE • Loose towel rack or soapdish? Tighten the screws. If it's still loose, then have the item moved so it can be fastened to an existing stud and the old holes patched.

• Ceramic soapdish fell out? Temporarily cover the gap with silver-colored duct tape so water won't get in. Have the broken one replaced with a soapdish of the same size.

Soapdish

Towel holder

These accessories are either screwed into the bathroom wall (preferably into a stud) or have a ceramic base that is cemented into the wall along with tile.

For safety's sake, each end of a grab bar must be attached to a stud (a wooden structural support behind the wall) or wood blocking between the studs. Grab bars can be mounted vertically (right) or horizontally.

Grab bar

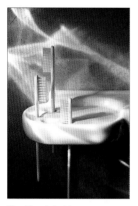

Toothbrush holder

Toilet paper holder

TUB FAUCETS/ ACCESSORIES

American Standard . 800-223-0068

Delta Faucet 800-345-3358

GROHE 630-582-7711

Kohler 800-456-4537

Moen 800-289-6636

Interbath (Ondine) . 800-423-9485

St. Thomas
Creations 800-536-2284

Waterworks 800-927-2120

SHOWERS

A shower can make or break your day. So make it a good one. Shower stalls are either ready-made units (in various sizes) or custom-built. Most ready-made shower-stall units consist of three walls, a glass door, and a floor pan. They are typically made of fiberglass, but they are available in new and costlier materials like Swanstone. The latest shower stalls often incorporate shampoo shelves, grab bars, seats, and even tiny storage cabinets with sliding doors. One-piece shower units can also come with an integral tub. They are 6' high by 5' wide, so measure your bathroom to make sure the unit will fit and match the location of your plumbing lines. Some manufacturers offer units with three detachable wall sections for easier installation in small bathrooms.

The advantage of building your own shower stall is that you can go as big or small as you wish. All you need are plumbing lines. The plumber will plumb the shower and create a shower pan with drain; the tile setter will cover the pan and walls with water-resistant material, such as tile or marble; and the contractor will install glass doors.

Some standard-size acrylic shower pans: the triangle is 48" across, the square is 36" and the rectangle 60". If you are building your own shower, you can also have a pan custom-made to fit any space.

Neo Angle shower enclosures like this one are ideal for tight spaces.

Folding glass doors (above) are available without metal tracks. Glass doors should be tempered safety glass with an anodized (rust-resistant) frame.

 TROUBLE • Mold in the grout? Clean with an anti-mold cleanser, then reseal the grout with a silicone sealant, available at most hardware stores.

• Uneven shower flow? The showerhead is clogged. Unscrew the showerhead and soak it in vinegar to remove mineral deposits. Use a toothpick to clear out clogged holes.

 CHECKLIST SHOWERHEADS ✔ Invest in a good showerhead. Top-of-the-line showerheads are made of solid brass—their weight should give them away. Standard showerheads offer only one type of spray. The more expensive ones have a number of settings, for example, needle sprays or pulsating massage.

SHOWER STALLS

Aqua Glass 800-632-0911
ASB (Trayco) 800-355-2721
Kohler 800-456-4537
Maax USA
Handicapped 800-625-6229

SHOWERHEADS

Kohler 800-456-4537
Interbath 800-423-9485
Speakman Co. 800-537-2107
Teledyne
(ShowerMassage). . . 800-525-2774

LIGHTING

Good lighting is the secret to looking good. For successful grooming, as well as convenience and safety, bathrooms should have *ambient lighting* (general illumination) as well as *task lighting* (lights that focus on specific areas, such as the sink, mirror, and tub/shower).

For the sink and mirror area, you want light that shines on you, not on the mirror. Makeup lights (a strip of metal or wood that anchors several lightbulbs), when placed over the mirror, are particularly effective as task lighting because the unshaded bulbs spread the light into the room and, more important, onto you. A pendant that hangs from a decorative chain from the ceiling over the sink can be a little too harsh and can cause shadows on the face. Sconces placed on either side of the mirror provide better overall light.

In the tub and shower area, get lights that are flush with the ceiling and vapor-resistant. Or install an exhaust fan that comes with a light and solve venting and lighting problems with one fixture—a good idea for small bathrooms.

Directional recessed lights (the round lights in the ceiling) are ideal for task lighting. Natural light from windows and a skylight are good sources of daytime ambient light.

TIME FACTOR

INSTALL	ELECTRICIAN'S TIME
Ceiling light	I hr
Strip (makeup) light	I hr

INSTALL	MIRROR HANGER'S TIME
Plate mirror (4' × 3')	I hr

MIRRORS

The mirrored medicine cabinet is the bathroom standard, even though the bathroom is the last place you should store medicine, the dampness can ruin most medication. Use these cabinets only to store toiletries. (Store medicine up high in the hall closet, away from children.)

If your bathroom has a fair amount of flat wall (no bumps or cracks), consider covering it with plate mirror, available at most glass companies. Get mirror that's ¼" thick (not ⅛"), and have the glass company cut it to your specifications. The edges will be ground to eliminate the sharpness, but for a more decorative effect, have the mirror beveled so the edges slant down to make a border. Plate mirror should be installed by mirror hangers. They will use both plastic clips that are screwed into the studs behind the wall and a special glass fixative (glue) smeared on the back of the mirror. Note: The fixative makes it tough to remove the mirror later on without damaging the wall surface and mirror.

• Framed mirrors, both antique and new, are effective and easy to install in small bathrooms.

• Mirrored tiles are relatively inexpensive and simple to apply, just make sure the wall is absolutely flat so that the tiles won't be uneven.

In small bathrooms, hang a mirrored cabinet (top right) or a framed mirror (bottom right).

VENTING

Because of steam generated by hot water, bathrooms should have vents that let out the moist air. Why? Because moisture can damage wood, paint, and/or wallpaper. Windows can double as vents, but in cold weather, open windows aren't a good idea. The best solution for window and windowless bathrooms is to install an exhaust fan in the ceiling directly above the shower or tub and vent the damp air to the outdoors—never into the attic. You can also get a vent-and-light combination, as shown above.

LIGHT SOURCES

Juno Lighting 800-367-5866

Lightolier 800-223-0726

NuTone, Inc. 800-543-8687

Thomas Lighting . . . 800-825-5844

MIRROR SOURCES

NuTone, Inc. 800-543-8687

St. Thomas
Creations 800-536-2284

Waterworks 800-927-2120

Sometimes you'll hear tiles described as being "wall" or "floor" tiles, but those descriptions can be confusing, as floor tiles can be put on walls or countertops. Some wall tiles, however, are not as durable as floor tiles and can't stand up to the abuse they'd get if installed on a floor. Floor tiles are typically sturdier than wall tiles (and usually more expensive), but that doesn't mean you can't put them on a wall or a sink countertop. Other lingo you need to know: *field* tiles are the ones that fill up most of a wall or a floor. *Trim* tiles have a decorative shape or a glazed edge; they're used along edges and corners. *Bullnose* tiles have one edge that is rounded to give a smooth finish to the top edge of wall tiles and backsplashes.

Installing tile is a two-step process. First, tiles are applied with adhesive to the substrate (wall or floor surface). (Floor tiles use thin-set mortar; wall tiles use premixed mastic adhesive.) Then, the spaces between the tiles are filled with grout. There are two basic types of grout: cement or epoxy. Grout cement is the standard. Epoxy is much more resistant to water and stains and, alas, much more expensive.

In big bathrooms, use the large 12"-square floor tiles to cut down on the number of grout lines. Smaller bathrooms are best tiled with smaller tiles, such as 6"-square floor tiles.

Decorative tiles (above) can cost from $2 to $100 each. Use standard tiles for most of the field and decorative tiles for accent and trim. To ensure a proper fit, the decorative tiles should be the same thickness and the same size as the field tiles.

 CHOOSING TILE AND GROUP

✔ Mixing field tiles from different manufacturers is risky because color, size, or thickness may vary.

✔ Not every line of field tiles has matching trim tiles, so decide how you'll edge the job before you buy field tiles.

✔ When choosing grout color, either match the tile color or go for a contrasting color. Dark-colored grout hides stains better than light-colored grout. For the highest durability and "cleanability," use epoxy grout.

✔ Always set aside up to 10 percent of your tile after a job is done for future repairs. Don't save excess grout (it has a short shelf-life). Write down the type and color of your grout and purchase fresh when you need it.

 TROUBLE • Stains in the grout? If cleaning solutions don't work, serious stains can be "painted" over with liquid grout colorant. You may need to paint all the grout for a color match.

• Big patches of broken grout? Call in the tile setter. A small patch? You can fix it yourself, but you'll need advice. Bring a broken chunk to a local tile dealer to help with color matching the new grout to the old. Then dig out the old grout with a grout saw, fill with new cement grout, let dry 24 hours, and seal with a silicone sealer.

TIME FACTOR

INSTALL	TILE SETTER'S TIME
Shower stall (floor and walls)	6 hrs
Bathtub wall	4 hrs

NOTE: Tile setters typically charge by the square foot. Most jobs require one day for drying before grout can be applied.

TILE MANUFACTURERS

American
Olean Tile 888-268-8453

Crossville Ceramics . 615-484-2110

Daltile 800-933-8453

Laufen Int'l. 800-758-8453

Summitville Tiles . . . 330-223-1511

U.S. Ceramic Tile . . . 800-321-0684

Florida Tile 800-352-8453

WALLS/FLOORS

Wood floors (see page 26) add a feeling of richness and warmth to the bath, especially when finished with baseboard molding and chair railing.

When it comes to bathroom walls, steam is the enemy. It can peel paint and wallpaper right off the walls. When painting, use a moisture-barrier paint primer and high-quality semigloss paint. For wallpaper, only vinyl will survive well. (See page 32 for paint, and page 84 for wallpaper.)

For floors, the main culprit is water, which makes carpeting problematic. Even industrial carpeting can get moldy. One flooring solution for bathrooms (and kitchens) is sheet vinyl. The material comes in 12'-wide sheets and unlimited length, so it can be installed in most bathrooms without dirt-gathering, germ-harboring seams. Having fewer or no seams means that water will have that much harder a job getting past the flooring and into the subfloor below. Sheet vinyl is glued to the subfloor and isn't easy to remove.

Sheet vinyl is also available in the form of 1-foot-square tiles for do-it-yourselfers. The tiles are fairly simple to install, just be sure to abut the edges tightly against each other.

Ceramic floor tile (see page 114) is so durable and water-resistant, it usually beats out the other flooring choices. It's best to get tiles with a slip-resistant glaze. Bear in mind that ceramic floor tile holds a temperature longer than other floor coverings do. This means that when the bathroom is cold, the tile floor will stay cold for a while after the heat has come on. One solution is to install radiant heating under the bathroom floor. Better yet, get a bath mat.

TROUBLE •Need to replace a damaged vinyl tile? Soften the tile's adhesive backing with heat. Put a towel on the tile and iron it until it can be pried up with a putty knife. If heat doesn't work, try freezing the tile with dry ice, then shattering it with a hammer.

•Bubble in your sheet vinyl? It's probably due to water. Fix the leak, then pierce the bubble with a knife. Make a tiny slit and inject vinyl flooring adhesive. Use a rolling pin and press out the bubble.

SHORTCUTS •Window treatments in the bathroom are tricky. Don't use blinds; they are hard to clean. The best solution is curtains made of washable fabric sprayed with water repellent so they won't mildew.

•Usually, old sheet vinyl has to be ripped out before you can put down new. There are some new types of sheet vinyl that can go right over the existing vinyl. Check with your flooring supplier.

TIME FACTOR

INSTALL	FLOOR INSTALLER'S TIME
Sheet vinyl	3 hrs
PAINT	**PAINTER'S TIME**
Prime, paint, and trim	8 hrs

NOTE: Figures are for a 10' × 10' bathroom. (Painting needs one day to dry.)

Sheet vinyl and ceramic tile are tops when it comes to water resistance.

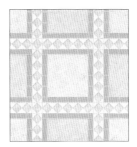

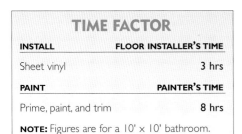

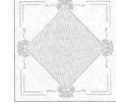

Most vinyl tiles have textured or embossed surfaces to help hide wear and tear, such as scuff marks. Vinyl tile comes in 12" squares and 9" x 12" squares.

VINYL FLOORING MANUFACTURERS

Armstrong	800-233-3823
Congoleum	800-934-3567
Domco	800-465-4030
Forbo Industries	800-342-0604
Tarkett	800-367-8275
Mannington Resilient Floors	800-356-6787

T he attic is more than just a place to store old junk—it's a little ecosystem. If it's working right, it should keep your roof healthy and your heating and cooling bills within reason.

ATTIC/ROOF

ATTIC/ROOF

Use this easy number guide to locate and identify all the parts of your roof and attic; explanations appear on the following pages.

ATTIC

1 . . . RIDGE BOARD

2 . . . RAFTERS

3 . . . CEILING JOISTS

4 . . . INSULATION
(on attic floor)

5 . . . DORMER

ROOF

6 . . . DECK SHEATHING

7 . . . ROOFING FELT

8 . . . ICE SHIELD

9 . . . SHINGLES

10 . . . VALLEY (with flashing)

11 . . . FLASHING

12 . . . FASCIA (behind gutter)

13 . . . RAKE BOARD

14 . . . SOFFIT (under eave)

VENTS

15 . . . ROOF VENT
(with flashing)

16 . . . PLUMBING VENT
(with flashing)

17 . . . GABLE VENT

GUTTERS

18 . . . GUTTER

19 . . . DOWNSPOUT

20 . . . STRAP

21 . . . ELBOW

22 . . . SPLASH BLOCK

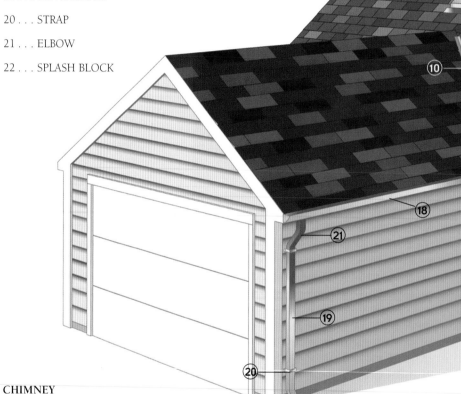

CHIMNEY

23 . . . CHIMNEY STACK

24 . . . CAP

25 . . . CHIMNEY FLASHING

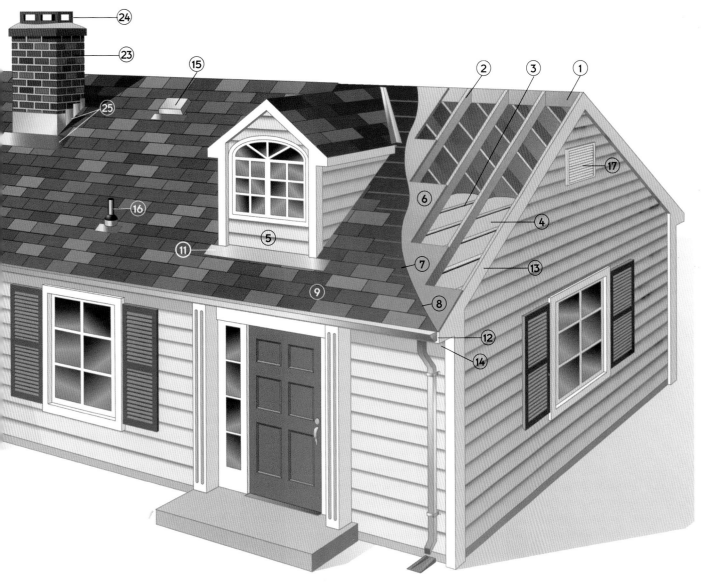

INSULATION

The high cost of heating in winter and cooling in summer demands that your house have proper insulation. An important area to insulate is the outer walls. Here, before drywall is applied, batts of fiberglass insulation have been fitted between the studs.

It's a cruel law of physics, but when it's cold out, the toasty warm air inside the house wants to go outside. And when it's hot outside, the heat wants to get inside. What's a homeowner to do? Put in insulation, that's what. Insulation slows this transfer of heat. In fact, like glass, wood, and other materials found in the home, insulation is rated by its R-value—its ability to resist the transfer of heat. The higher the R-value, the better its insulating qualities.

Insulation is made of cellulose, fiberglass, rock wool, or synthetics and it comes in batts, blankets, rigid foam boards, or bags of loose fill. You can't see insulation from the lived-in areas of your house because it's covered by drywall. You know it's there, however, because your air-conditioning and heating bills aren't sky-high. You can get a glimpse of it in unfinished spaces, such as the basement or attic.

Where does insulation go? For the past 40 years or so, whenever a house has been built, batts of insulation have been fitted around joists in the attic floor and the basement ceiling, and installed between studs in the outside walls before the drywall is put in place.

Rigid foam board insulation, made of polystyrene or urethane, is used over foundation walls, beneath vinyl and aluminum siding, or under flat roofs. It is flammable and must be covered with fire-resistant material, such as drywall or siding, at least ½" thick.

INSULATION SMART

✔Check your local building code for the recommended insulation R-values for the various parts of your house.

✔Buy insulation according to R-value, not thickness.

✔Have blanket insulation installed in open areas and batts put in where a lot of cutting must be done.

✔The side of the insulation facing the interior of the house is lined with foil to protect it from condensation. The foil should face the heated side of the wall.

✔When loose-fill insulation is blown in, make sure the contractor uses enough to counteract its natural tendency to settle.

The depth of this layer of loose-fill insulation is determined by the severity of the climate.

TIME FACTOR

INSTALL	CONTRACTOR'S TIME
Batt insulation	2½ hrs
Loose fill	1½ hrs
Rigid foam board	1 hr

NOTE: Installation is for a 20' × 20' area.

ATTIC VENTS

A ventilated attic is the secret to a long-lasting roof. Hot attic air can build up and warp the attic shingles, while moisture from the house below can create condensation inside the attic, causing insulation—and the surrounding wood—to deteriorate. Attic vents work in tandem, the exhaust vent is placed high in the attic to exhaust hot air and moisture; the intake vent is placed lower and pulls in outside air. Two exhaust vent oldies are the *roof* vent, a raised rectangular box and the *cupola*, which looks like a small house with slatted sides perched on the roof. The newer exhaust vent is the *ridge* vent—a slit along the length of the roof's ridge that is then covered with roofing material. Two popular intake vents are the *gable* vent, a louvered screen installed in the attic's wall and a *soffit* or *under-eave* vent (a metal grill fitted into slots cut into the eaves).

Maximize the effectiveness of a gable vent by installing a power attic ventilator behind it.

 TROUBLE •Supercold walls in your old house? Check how much insulation there is. Remove switch plates and outlet covers on exterior walls and look inside the openings—don't forget to turn off the electricity to the outlet boxes before probing (see page 140). If the insulation layer is thin, or if the loose fill has settled very low inside the walls, a contractor can make holes in the drywall and blow in loose fill between the studs.

•No insulation in your old house? If you can't insulate everything at once, prioritize: insulate the attic floor to save the most on fuel bills; after that, install insulated windows (see pages 82–83); insulate the walls last.

INSULATION MANUFACTURERS

Celotex Corp. 800-556-4215

CertainTeed. 610-341-7000

Dow Plastics 800-441-4369

Johns Manville 800-654-3103

Owens Corning. . . . 800-438-7465

ROOF MATERIALS

A dark gray slate roof like this one is extremely durable, but the material is heavy. Small guard lips are sometimes installed along the edge to prevent any slates that have worked loose from falling and possibly injuring someone below.

As any skier knows, layering one's clothing is a good defense against the weather. The same rule applies to roofs. Underneath a roof's surface are several layers. The first is called sheathing, and it consists of plywood panels laid over the rafters of the roof. The next layer is made of asphalt-impregnated felt. Finally, roofing material is installed over the felt. Leaks in the roof usually result from worn or broken materials.

When it comes to choosing roofing materials, there are a number of things to consider: cost, looks, and durability. Slate and tile last the longest—up to 100 years—and they are the most expensive. Cedar shingles and the rough-cut, thicker cedar shakes can last from 10 to 40 years if they are treated with a preservative every five years. The most common shingles, asphalt/fiberglass, are the least expensive and last at least 20 years.

A warm gold color at first, cedar shingles and shakes fade to a soft gray.

Asphalt/fiberglass shingles come in an extensive variety of colors.

Roofs made from red or tan ceramic clay tiles are very strong and durable.

 CHECKLIST HIRING A ROOFER

To find a good roofer, ask at building-supply yards or the building inspector's office.

✔ Get written bids with time schedules, and a written guarantee, from three different roofers. Make sure they specify materials by brand name and features.

✔ Check to see that all bids cover the same specifications. Don't hire on price alone. Get references and call them (see page 17). Look at other jobs the roofer has done.

✔ Be sure the roofer obtains all the necessary building permits. Check his insurance and your homeowners insurance to make sure that any potential claims will be covered.

✔ Before installing a cedar roof, check the local building code. Some communities ban wood roofs as fire hazards.

 SHORTCUTS

• In areas with cold winters, a roof's felt layer should have a 30" ice shield around its lower edges. The shield makes a watertight seal around roofing nails so that if melting ice and snow backs up under the shingles, creating an ice dam, the ice shield will protect the roof.

• Before reroofing with asphalt/fiberglass shingles, find out whether there's a layer of older shingles below the ones that are already on the roof. If there's no other layer, new shingles can be nailed over the old.

• If the existing roof is being removed, make sure the roofers inspect the sheathing underneath and repair any damage.

• Partially lifted or curled asphalt shingles are a sign of excessive heat in the attic. You need attic ventilation pronto.

TIME FACTOR

REPLACE	ROOFER'S TIME
Wood shingles	5 days
Asphalt	5 days
Clay tile	6 days
Slate	6 days

NOTE: Estimates are for a 2,000-sq.-ft. roof and include time for installation of a new layer of felt.

ROOFING MATERIALS RESOURCES

ASPHALT/FIBERGLASS

Bird, Inc. 800-247-3462

Celotex Corp. 800-662-4609

CertainTeed Corp. . 800-345-1145

Georgia Pacific 800-284-5347

Owens Corning . . . 800-438-7465

CLAY

Celadon
Ceramic Slate 800-235-7528

Maruhachi
Ceramics 800-736-6221

SLATE

Evergreen Slate 518-642-2530

New England Slate . 888-637-5283

WOOD

Cedar Shake and
Shingle Bureau 800-843-3578

Clarke Group 800-963-3388

FLASHING/GUTTERS

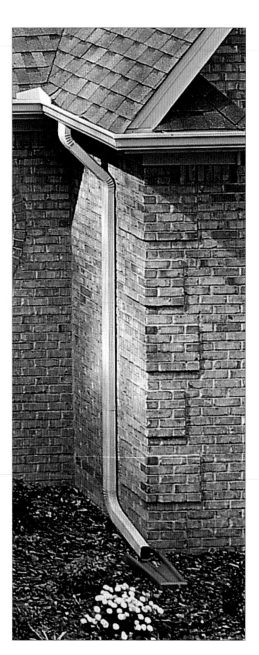

Most roofs are pitched like tents to direct water into the gutters, where it is then funneled into the downspouts. Modern gutter systems are usually made of aluminum, vinyl, or a galvanized metal. Unless the gutters are cleared of debris in spring and fall, water may overflow from them and pool around the house. From there it can seep into the basement or even splash up and work its way through windows or cracks in the house's siding. The moral of the story? Keep your gutters clean.

The roofing materials will protect the roof from water, but how are roof joints and the areas around a chimney and vents protected? Enter flashing—strips of copper or aluminum sheeting that are nailed along roof joints and around chimneys and vents to help keep those vulnerable spots watertight. Roof leaks are often the result of worn or poorly laid flashing.

TIME FACTOR	
REPAIR	**ROOFER'S TIME**
Flashing	2–5 hrs
INSTALL	**CONTRACTOR'S TIME**
Gutters	6 hrs
NOTE: Time estimate is for 40'.	

Gutters and downspouts (or leaders as they are called in some parts) carry the water runoff a safe distance away from the house so it won't undermine the foundation. Gutters must be flexible enough to expand and contract as the temperature fluctuates and watertight enough to fend off leaks.

GUTTER SMART

✔ Gutters usually hang from the roof or fascia board by straps or brackets that are placed at 3' to 4' intervals.

✔ Gutter pieces are sold in various lengths that can slide together to create overlaps. Gutters are usually 4" wide, but large roofs should have gutters 5" or 6" wide. Seamless gutters can be made on-site by siding contractors using machinery that extrudes aluminum gutters in lengths to exactly match the roof's edges.

✔ The point where gutter and downspout meet is vulnerable to clogs from leaves and debris. To keep the downspout drain hole running free, cover it with a downspout guard or strainer.

✔ Downspouts should be secured against the sides of the house by metal straps placed at 6' intervals.

Gutter helmets, like the one shown here, cover gutters to keep out debris. Gutter screens are another effective way to prevent clogs with little maintenance.

Flashing is especially important for protecting the joint between the chimney and the roof because the chimney moves independently of the house.

 TROUBLE

• Pin-size holes in the flashing? Daub them with roofing cement to seal them.

• Sagging gutter? Use pliers to twist the strap nearest the sag to shorten it.

• Can't find anyone to clean the gutters? You can buy an extension for a garden hose; hook it over the gutters and flush them out while you stand on the ground.

• Weird depression in the ground underneath a gutter? That's a sign of an overflowing gutter. Check for a clogged downspout that might be causing the overflow.

• A clean gutter, yet water's still not draining? The gutter's slope may be too shallow. Increase the gutter's pitch to ¼" per 4'.

GUTTER PRODUCT RESOURCES

Alcoa 800-621-7466

American Metal
Products. 800-669-3190

Benjamin Obdyke . . 800-346-7655

CHIMNEYS

W hat does a chimney do any-way? This tall, hollow pillar of bricks or stones directs the smoke and gases created by combustion in a fireplace (see page 68) or furnace (see page 136) away from the house so it won't burn down.

In modern fireplaces the flue (the hollow part of the chimney) is built with a lining made of clay flue tile, concrete flue tile, or prefabricated steel. If the chimney on your house is older, its lining may be cracked. Such cracking not only poses a dangerous fire hazard, it also can create a health risk by allowing deadly carbon monoxide to seep into the house. If the damage is not too extensive, it can be patched by a mason. If the damage is severe, have the chimney relined. (Another option: have a specialty contractor insert a wood-burning stove into the fireplace and install a suitable metal flue inside the chimney.)

Because a masonry chimney is so heavy, it needs its own foundation. The whole structure naturally settles independently of the house, causing the joints between chimney and roof to shift. Don't worry—it's normal. To prevent rainwater and melting snow from leaking through these joints, they are sealed with sheets of metal flashing on all sides of the chimney that intersect with the roof (see pages 126-127).

Non-masonry chimneys that are attached to the side of the house, like the one shown here, usually service a gas furnace or a prefab fireplace.

SHORTCUTS • Remove soot from glazed fireplace tiles with a mixture of lemon juice and salt, then wash with water. Don't try this on brick, though, because it is porous.

• Inspect your chimney inside the house wherever its pillar is visible—usually in the attic. Ask someone to burn damp rags in the fireplace while you observe the pillar of the chimney in the attic. If you see smoke, don't build another fire until the chimney and its lining have been repaired by a professional.

The top of a chimney should be capped, as shown here, to keep out rain.

CHIMNEY CLEANING

 CHECKLIST ✔ When fuel burns in the furnace, it creates soot, which sticks to the inside of the chimney. Have your heating service contractor clean out the chimney annually when he comes to check the furnace.

✔ When wood burns, it deposits creosote, a gummy, tarlike substance, inside the chimney. Creosote can ignite and create dangerous chimney fires. Check your chimney every fall for creosote buildup. Shine a flashlight up the flue; if you find tarry-looking deposits, have it cleaned without delay.

✔ Hire a professional, licensed, fully insured chimney sweep (or a heating contractor if the chimney serves your furnace). He'll block off all the flue openings into the house, clean the creosote from the whole length of the chimney, and vacuum it away. Chimney sweeps generally offer free estimates.

TROUBLE • Crumbling mortar in the firebox? If neglected, damaged mortar can be a fire hazard. It is easily fixed by having it repacked (or repointed) with new mortar.

• Cracked chimney bricks? Water and freezing temperatures can eventually shatter brick. Any that are broken, cracked, or missing should be replaced before you build a fire.

• Leaks in the walls next to the chimney? Damaged flashing around the chimney can be the culprit. Have a roofer repair the flashing.

TIME FACTOR	
INSTALL	**MASON'S TIME**
Masonry chimney	3–7 days
CLEAN	**SWEEP'S TIME**
Chimney	3 hrs

A wire spark arrester fits over the opening of the chimney to keep sparks from igniting your roof or your neighbor's roof.

CHIMNEY RESOURCES

Brick Institute
of America 703-620-0010

Chimney Safety Institute
of America 800-536-0118

Hearth Products
Assoc. (tech dept.) . . 703-522-0086

National Chimney
Sweep Guild 301-963-5600

Superior Clay Corp. 614-922-4122

BASEMENT

Yes, it's dark and musty, but the basement is home to several vital systems—heating, hot water, and electrical—that keep you happy and comfortable. So go on down there and check them out. This chapter will give you a quick primer on how they work.

BASEMENT

Becoming basement smart is simple with this look-and-learn guide to help you locate and identify some of the major systems that make your house work. Find out more on the following pages.

FOUNDATION

1 . . . WALL

2 . . . CONCRETE FLOOR

3 . . . STEEL PIPE COLUMN

4 . . . SUPPORT BEAM

5 . . . HOPPER VENT WINDOW

6 . . . JOIST

7 . . . SUMP

8 . . . SUMP PUMP (inside sump)

FORCED-AIR HEATING SYSTEM

9 . . . FURNACE

10 . . . HOT-AIR PLENUM

11 . . . OUTGOING AIR DUCT

12 . . . RETURN AIR DUCT

13 . . . SHUTOFF SWITCH

14 . . . ACCESS DOOR

15 . . . FILTER (not seen)

16 . . . EXHAUST FLUE

17 . . . CHIMNEY

18 . . . OIL STORAGE TANK

WATER HEATER

19 . . . WATER HEATER

20 . . . COLD WATER SUPPLY PIPE

21 . . . COLD WATER SHUTOFF VALVE

22 . . . OUTGOING HOT WATER PIPE

23 . . . TEMPERATURE CONTROL

ELECTRICAL SYSTEM

24 . . . MAIN ELECTRICAL LINE

25 . . . MAIN SHUTOFF SWITCH

26 . . . SERVICE PANEL

27 . . . CIRCUIT BREAKERS

28 . . . CIRCUIT LINES

29 . . . ELECTRICAL OUTLET

LAUNDRY

30 . . WASHER

31 . . . LAUNDRY SINK

32 . . . DRAIN HOSE

33 . . . DRYER

34 . . . DRYER VENT PIPE

BASEMENT STAIRWAY

35 . . . STRINGER

36 . . . TREAD

37 . . . HANDRAIL

38 . . . BALUSTER

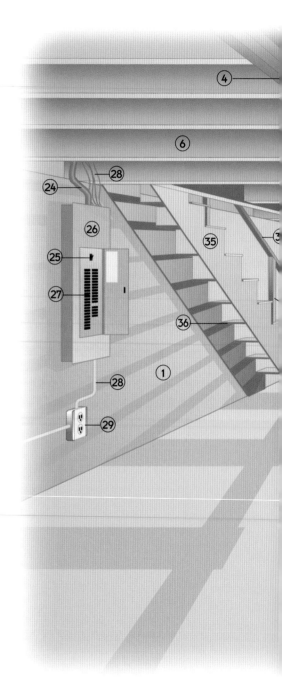

SMART
GUIDE

FOUNDATION

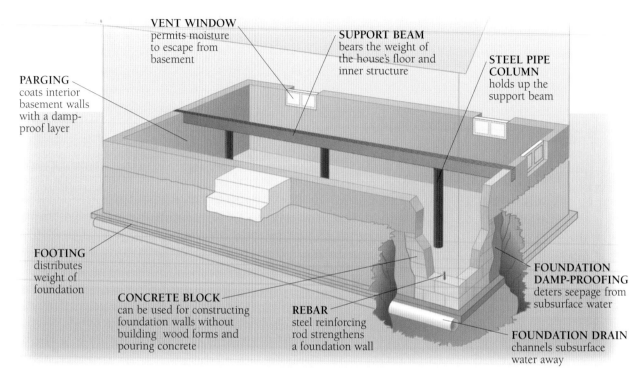

VENT WINDOW permits moisture to escape from basement

SUPPORT BEAM bears the weight of the house's floor and inner structure

STEEL PIPE COLUMN holds up the support beam

PARGING coats interior basement walls with a damp-proof layer

FOOTING distributes weight of foundation

CONCRETE BLOCK can be used for constructing foundation walls without building wood forms and pouring concrete

REBAR steel reinforcing rod strengthens a foundation wall

FOUNDATION DAMP-PROOFING deters seepage from subsurface water

FOUNDATION DRAIN channels subsurface water away

Foundations widen at their lower edges to form underground concrete platforms called footings. This extra width distributes the weight of the house over a greater area.

Believe it or not, this is probably the most important part of your house or addition. A foundation must be able to withstand the seasonal expansion and contraction of the earth underneath it, or else major cracks in the floor or walls of the basement can develop. Major bad news.

What are foundations made of? In old houses these partially buried walls were often built from stones or brick mortared together. Newer foundations are built with mortared concrete blocks or poured concrete. They are reinforced with steel bars called rebars.

How deep does a foundation have to be? That depends on where you live and the depth at which the ground could freeze—known as the frost line. In mild climates, all that's needed is a slab of concrete at ground level. Where temperatures regularly dip below freezing, foundation walls of concrete block should reach below the frost line. The colder the climate, the deeper the frost line—in some states it's 4' deep or more. At that point, builders usually go another few feet down so they can get a full basement out of the deal—a little extra digging doesn't cost that much more.

Why so much worry about the frost line? Because the soil *above* the frost line freezes and thaws, creating movement. If any parts of your house are above the frost line—for example, front steps, or porch or deck footings—they can heave and crack.

CHECKLIST: BASEMENT PROTECTION

✔ Keep the basement dry. How? 1) Make sure the soil around the foundation slopes down and away from the house (this is called "grading"). If your house is in a valley and the soil can't be graded, then install a gravel trench or an underground drainpipe around the house to help funnel water away. 2) Fix gutters and leaders so they carry water at least 10' away from the foundation.

✔ Install a dehumidifier in a damp basement to avoid any mold or mildew problems.

✔ Watch out for termites and other pests that breed in the soil. Make sure all wood structures on the outside of the house are at least 8" above the ground. Stack firewood away from the house.

✔ Have small cracks patched with acrylic cement to seal out water. (You can do it yourself. The stuff comes in easy-to-use tubes, available at most hardware stores.)

TIME FACTOR

BUILD	CONCRETE WORKER'S TIME
30' × 50' × 8'	7 days in summer 14 days in winter
REPAIR	**CONCRETE WORKER'S TIME**
Small crack	1 hr to 1 day

SUMP PUMPS

It happens: excessive rain or snow, overflowing rivers, or even a neighbor's leaking swimming pool can flood your basement. Don't panic. Buy or rent a sump pump. It tackles the water at the sump—a pit 1'–2' deep built into a corner of many modern basements. The sump pump empties water into a hose or pipe leading to a dry well or a street gutter. There are two types of sump pumps: submersible and pedestal. Note: If water in your basement is a chronic problem, install a permanent sump pump. It will kick on when water reaches a certain level and whisk it away through its own drainpipe.

This submersible sump pump sits in the basement sump pit. A plastic pipe connects to the pump to conduct water out through a basement window or door.

Foundation walls are usually strengthened with internal steel reinforcing bars, called rebars, that fit through the holes in these masonry blocks. The holes can then be filled with poured concrete.

FOUNDATION RESOURCES

Concrete Foundation
Assoc. 319-895-6940

Int'l Concrete
Repair Institute 703-450-0116

Portland Cement
Assoc. 847-966-6200

SUMP PUMP MANUFACTURERS

Flotec 800-365-6832

Hilo Ind. 800-928-7867

Simer Pump 800-468-7867

Wayne Pump 800-237-0987

HEATING SYSTEM

It's really quite simple: your house gets warm by converting oil, gas, or electricity into heat, then distributing that heat throughout the house—or just to the room or zone you want warmed. This magic is performed by the heating system. There are several types:

With a *forced-air furnace*, a blower in the furnace pushes heated air through a network of metal ducts. (These ducts also serve to push cold air through if you have central air-conditioning.) The ducts extend from the furnace to grill-covered openings (or registers) in the floors, walls, or ceilings of each room. As the air cools, it returns through other metal openings connected to ducts that lead back to the furnace, where it will be filtered, heated, and circulated again.

A *hydronic boiler* works by heating water in a tank called, for good reason, a boiler. The hot water is then pumped through a system of pipes to radiators in each room where the heat from the water warms the air in the room. There are two types: circulating hot water and steam. If the radiator has two pipes going into the floor, it's a circulating system; if it has one pipe, it's steam.

Electric baseboard heaters generate heat by sending electricity through resistant wiring. Although inexpensive to install,

Most oil or gas furnaces are equipped with electronic ignition. If the furnace goes out, press the restart button.

A hydronic boiler, like the one shown here, is less drying than a forced-air furnace. That's good news for people with dry skin and allergies who can use a little extra humidity in the air during winter.

they are practical only where electricity is relatively cheap.

How does a heating system turn itself off and on? It's controlled by a thermostat mounted on a room's interior wall. The thermostat measures the room's temperature and either fires up or shuts off the furnace, depending on what's needed to maintain the temperature you've set. The most efficient systems divide a house into zones, each with its own thermostat. Note: Be sure a thermostat is not installed near a fireplace or anyplace where it will be in direct sunlight; its reading will be inaccurate.

SHORTCUTS • High heating bills mean either poor insulation (see p. 122) or a lazy furnace. Some furnaces can be retrofitted with new, high-efficiency burners; others may need to be replaced. A new furnace should pay for itself in savings on fuel. Check with your fuel supplier for more information about fuel savings.

• Install a programmable electronic thermostat. It lets you preset temperatures for any time or day of the week, so that the furnace turns off as you leave the house for work and comes back on an hour before you get home. No more cranking up the heat, so you spend less money on fuel and have an evenly warm house when you need it.

TROUBLE • No heat? Check the thermostat setting. Then look at the main electrical panel for a tripped circuit breaker or blown fuse (even gas and oil furnaces need electricity for pumps and fans). Push the reset button. If that doesn't work, call your fuel supplier to check the furnace.

• Smell fuel or smoke? *Beware—fuel or exhaust fumes signal the threat of an explosion.* Immediately shut down the furnace at the main on/off switch (usually placed at the top of the basement stairs or inside the garage).

• Allergies or asthma? Replace the standard air filter on your forced-air furnace with a high-efficiency air cleaner.

Safety Note: A furnace vents through a chimney; a clogged one can result in a build-up of carbon monoxide—a deadly natural by-product of furnace combustion. You can't detect it yourself because it's a colorless, odorless gas. Install a carbon monoxide detector on a basement ceiling or wall.

A clogged filter, like the one protruding from this forced-air furnace, adds to fuel bills. Wash or replace it every 4–6 weeks during the heating season.

FURNACE MANUFACTURERS

ELECTRIC BASEBOARD

Cadet Mfg.	800-442-2338
Marley Electric Co.	803-479-4006
TPI Corp.	800-251-0382

FORCED-AIR

Carrier	800-422-7743
Lennox	800-953-6669
Rheem	800-548-7433

HYDRONIC BOILER

Burnham Corp.	717-397-4701
Slant/Fin Corp.	516-484-2600
Weil-McLain	219-879-6561

WATER HEATER

The thermostat of a water heater allows you to choose the temperature of your hot water.

Hot running water at the turn of a faucet is for many of us the high point of civilization. But how does it get there? The main water pipe that brings water from your well or the town's water line splits into two lines when it enters your house. One line supplies the house with cold water and the other leads to a water heater. Whenever you turn on a hot-water faucet, hot water leaves the water heater (pushing a slug of cool water through the pipes ahead of it), and the heater starts warming more water to replenish the supply.

How does the water get hot? Electric hot-water heaters warm it with heating elements located inside the tank. Gas and oil models heat by means of a flame beneath the tank. If your heating system has a boiler, it may have a coil of pipe located inside it that heats water for your personal use before sending it out in a separate plumbing system leading to bathroom and kitchen faucets.

There may be another tank in your basement besides the water heater. If you get your water from a well (instead of from a municipal water supply), then you'll find a large holding tank for well water. An electric well pump buried deep in the ground forces well water into the tank, where enough water pressure is maintained for use on demand. Gauges at the front of the tank allow you to monitor the pressure inside.

The name plate on any water heater lists its specifications: gallon capacity, power rating, recovery rate (gallons heated per hour), and height.

SHORTCUTS
• You can make your water heater more energy-efficient by wrapping it in a jacket of fiberglass insulation. Wrap kits are available at home centers and hardware stores.

• Water heaters incorporate a pressure-relief valve to prevent dangerous pressure buildup in the tank. Check the valve's safety lever every few months to make sure that it's working properly.

• Check for rust at the base of the water heater. If it's very rusty, replace the tank before it springs a leak.

• If your water heater is powered separately from the furnace, save money and turn the furnace off during the summer.

• To avoid burns from scalding water—especially if there are children or guests in the house—set the control on the water heater thermostat no higher than 120°.

CENTRAL AIR-CONDITIONING

Central air uses air ducts to circulate cool air through each room of the house. It has two units: the noisy one, called the compressor, that sits outdoors and the one inside the basement, called

the air handler. (The air handler can be part of a forced-air heating system.) Tubes connect the two, carrying the all-important refrigerant (liquid stuff that cools air) back and forth. The outside unit chills the liquid and sends it to the air handler, which then blows newly cooled air through air ducts connected to each room in the house. (In a forced-air furnace, the same ducts used for heating are used for cooling.) Central air kicks in when the thermostat signals the need to chill out.

TIME FACTOR

	PLUMBER'S TIME
Replace water heater	4 hrs
Clean/service water heater	1-2 hrs
HVAC CONTRACTOR'S TIME	
Replace Central Air Unit	1-1½ days
Clean/Service	1-2 hrs

NOTE: HVAC stands for Heating, Ventilation, and Air Conditioning

TROUBLE
• No hot water? Push the reset button to fire up the heater. If that doesn't do it, call your fuel provider or furnace contractor. If you have gas, check the pilot light; if it's out, call your gas supplier.

• Running out of hot water all the time? Your water heater is too small to meet your household needs. Have it replaced with a larger unit.

• Tepid water? Sediment can build up in the tank over time and reduce the heating element's effectiveness. Have a plumber drain the tank and flush out any harmful sediment.

WATER HEATER MANUFACTURERS

Amtrol Inc.
(Boiler-Mate) 401-884-6300

A.O. Smith 800-527-1953

Rheem 800-432-8373

CENTRAL AIR SOURCES

Carrier 800-422-7743

York Int'l. 717-771-6418

TRADE
Air Conditioning and
Refrigeration Inst. . . 703-524-8800

ELECTRICAL SYSTEM

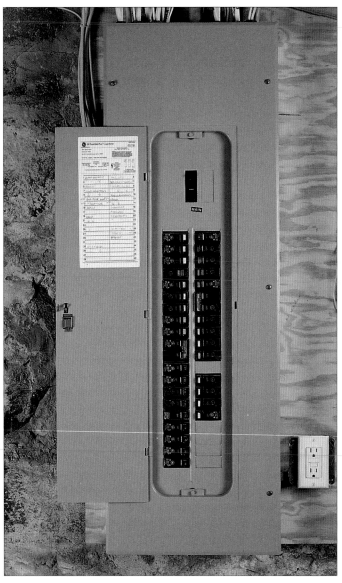

The circuit breakers should be labeled (by room or appliance) to make it easier to identify and repair problems with each circuit. The spaces without breakers (expansion blanks) are for future electrical additions.

Open that gray metal cabinet door called the service panel and the secrets of your home's electrical system will unfold. The panel is usually mounted on a basement or garage wall, so bring a flashlight. See the big wire leading into it? It's the line that connects your house to your local utility company. Inside the panel, at the top, you'll see a switch called the main service disconnect—it shuts off all the power to your house. Below that, you'll find rows of switches called circuit breakers (or, in older houses, rows of glass fuses) that protect each circuit.

What's a circuit? It's a circle of wiring that supplies electricity to a room or an area of the house, such as the kitchen or living room, and then brings it back to the electrical panel. Circle...circuit, get it?

Think of an electrical circuit as a circular fence with the circuit breaker acting as a protective gate. When the gate is "closed," electricity flows through the circuit. But if there's a problem, such as an overload in the circuit, the breaker switches to "open," and the electricity is stopped to prevent a fire or shock hazard. Once the problem has been corrected, you simply switch the circuit breaker back to close the gate.

For your safety, your electrical panel and all electrical outlets and switches are grounded through a system of wires and bars that connect to a solid metal rod in the ground just outside the house. Why all the fuss? Because electricity is lazy; any weird zaps from lightning will safely follow the path of least resistance—namely the grounding rod—into the earth.

ELECTRICAL TERMS

Electricity flows round and round its circuit, much like the blood in our bodies. And like blood, which provides the power to move muscles, electricity powers our appliances and lights. In order for blood to circulate, it needs pressure to push it through the arteries. The same goes for electricity. The voltage is like blood pressure, amperage is similar to the size of the arteries, while the wattage is equivalent to blood volume. Here's more on these mystifying terms:

Amperage, or *amps*, refers to how much electricity can flow through a circuit—it is determined by the type and size of the electrical wiring. If the wire doesn't have room for all the amperage going through it, the circuit breaker shuts it down. Older homes are served by 60 amps, newer homes by 200.

Voltage, or *volts*, is the term for measuring the pressure pushing the electricity through a circuit. It can fluctuate from 110 to 120 volts for standard electrical fixtures and 220 to 240 volts for more energy-intensive items, such as the stove and dryer that require their own circuits and circuit breakers.

Wattage, or *watts*, equals the electric power that flows through a circuit. It is measured by multiplying the number of amps (the rate of flow) by the number of volts (the pressure pushing the flow). Among other things, your utility bill is based on the number of kilowatt-hours you use.

TIME FACTOR

INSTALL	ELECTRICIAN'S TIME
New circuit	3-7 hrs

REPAIR	ELECTRICIAN'S TIME
Faulty circuit	1-5 hrs

TROUBLE • Appliance doesn't work? It's either 1) a faulty appliance, 2) a bad outlet, or 3) an overloaded circuit. Plug a lamp into the outlet to see if it works. If it does, the appliance is faulty; if it doesn't, check the circuit breaker. If the breaker is tripped, turn it on. If it trips again, there's a "short" in the wiring or a problem in the outlet. Call an electrician to check it out immediately because a short circuit or a faulty outlet can cause a fire.

• Three-prong plug doesn't fit your two-holed outlet.? Don't dismantle or bend back the grounding prong—it's there to protect you from shock if the appliance or fixture has a short. And don't use an adapter plug; it can't protect you from shock. Best to have an electrician rewire the outlet.

GFCI EXPLAINED
It's called a Ground Fault Circuit Interrupter, or GFCI. It works like any regular outlet, except that it has a hyper-sensitive sensor built into it that trips at the merest hint of trouble. Since electricity and water make a deadly pair, electrical codes specify GFCIs for outlets near sinks in bathrooms and kitchens. If a GFCI trips, fix the problem that caused it to shut down, then turn the circuit back on by pushing the reset button in the center of the outlet.

ELECTRICAL TRADE ASSOCIATIONS

Independent Electrical Contractors, Inc. 800-456-4324

Nat'l. Electrical Contractors Assoc. 800-888-6322

National Electrical Manufacturers Assoc. 703-841-3200

Nat'l. Electrical Safety Foundation 703-841-3229

WASHER/DRYER

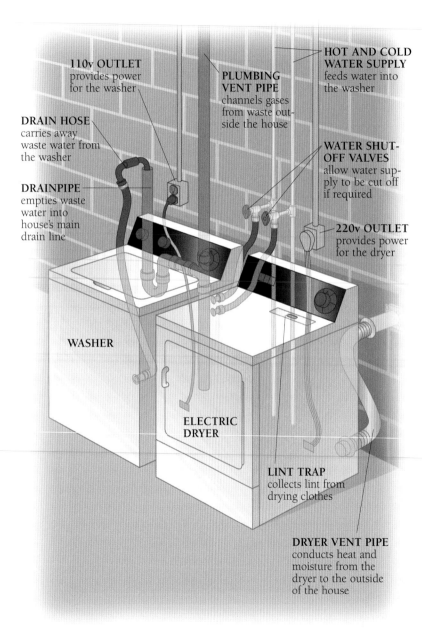

110v OUTLET
provides power
for the washer

DRAIN HOSE
carries away
waste water from
the washer

DRAINPIPE
empties waste
water into
house's main
drain line

**PLUMBING
VENT PIPE**
channels gases
from waste out-
side the house

**HOT AND COLD
WATER SUPPLY**
feeds water into
the washer

**WATER SHUT-
OFF VALVES**
allow water sup-
ply to be cut off
if required

220v OUTLET
provides power
for the dryer

WASHER

**ELECTRIC
DRYER**

LINT TRAP
collects lint from
drying clothes

DRYER VENT PIPE
conducts heat and
moisture from the
dryer to the outside
of the house

Washers and dryers are fre-
quently found where there's
the most room for them—in the
basement. Alas, this isn't the most convenient location. If you can, install these
babies on the same floor as the bedrooms, where the dirty clothes and
linens tend to accumulate. Look for
space in a closet near the bathroom,
because they need to be near a water
supply. (For that reason, another place to
check for space is near the kitchen.)

Of the two appliances, the dryer uses
the most power. It's plugged into an
odd-looking, three-slot outlet that connects directly to its own circuit breaker
in the main electrical panel. The shape
of the outlet prevents you from inserting anything but a dryer plug in it—a
good idea, considering that the dryer
outlet supplies 220 volts instead of the
standard 110 volts that comes from
regular outlets. A dryer also needs a
vent—a round sheet-metal or corrugat-
ed-plastic pipe—that leads from the
back of the dryer to the outdoors.

Washers need electricity, hot and cold
water lines (each with a separate shutoff valve), and a drain—all that water has
to go somewhere when the washer is
done with it. A large rubber drain hose
typically routes the water to a pipe that
leads to the house's main drainpipe. If
you want to move the washer from the
basement to the upstairs, it's relatively
easy to relocate the water supply, but
connecting the drain hose to the main
drain can be more difficult.

*When shopping for washers and dryers,
ask about the latest models that save on
energy and cut down on water usage.*

see below.

SHORTCUTS •If your dryer is in the basement, make sure it is located as far from the furnace as possible. Lint from the dryer can plug up the furnace air intake, increasing fuel consumption as well as causing a hazardous condition that might lead to a fire.

•Dryer vent pipes that are long and have sharp bends are difficult to clean. The shorter the vent pipe and the less bends it has, the better. Clean it out once a year; see below.

TROUBLE •Clothes taking forever to dry? 1) The dryer's lint trap might be clogged. That's easily remedied by sliding the trap out of the dryer and peeling off the blanket of lint coating the inside of it. 2) If the problem persists, the vent pipe might be clogged. First disconnect the pipe and then clear it with a straightened coat hanger. Don't forget to check the outside screen covering the vent outlet. Note: A plugged vent pipe is a fire hazard.

•Does the washer take a long time to fill? Shut off the water by turning off the shutoff valves. Remove both rubber hoses on the back of the washer. In the end of each hose, or on the washer itself, you'll find small filters that get clogged up with dirt and debris. Clean the filters, replace the hoses, turn on the water and check for leaks, then get back to your washing.

Space-saving stackable washer-dryer combos can fit into narrow closets and mudrooms.

WATER SOFTENER

If your water is laden with minerals that make it "hard," you can route it through a water softener. It removes minerals from water by filtering it through resin beads coated with sodium or potassium chloride, a.k.a. salt. The salt must be replenished every 3–6 months.

TIME FACTOR

REPLACE	SERVICE TIME
Washer	½ hr
Dryer	½ -1 hr

NOTE: Repairs are covered under the warranty of the appliance.

WASHER/DRYERS MANUFACTURERS

Amana	800-843-0304
Frigidaire	800-685-6005
GE	800-626-2000
Maytag	800-688-9900
Whirlpool	800-253-1301

REC ROOM

You'd never know it was a basement thanks to the covered steel columns and suspended ceiling which allow for a generous number of recessed lights.

Most basements are born as dark, dank spaces suited for little more than keeping the furnace hidden. But a basement can be made over into a great activity space useful for everything from a playroom for your kids to a rehearsal space for your R & B band.

Before a basement can be useful, though, it must be dry (see page 135). Have any cracks patched with mortar or hydraulic cement (a cement that seals out water), and the walls and floor coat-ed with a waterproof sealer. (If you still have moisture problems after that, consult a foundation contractor; your foundation may need major repairs.)

Develop a good plan if you want the basement to look like a real room. You'll be sharing the space with the furnace and water heater, and building codes are quite strict about how these units can be concealed. It may be smart to ask a foundation contractor for help.

Begin your "new" basement with a new floor. Sure, you can simply lay durable carpet over the cement slab, but consider "floating" a floor system over it—you'll end up with a warmer floor that's easier on your feet. The contractor nails a network of wood slats, called "sleepers," to the slab and wedges rigid insulation between them. Then plywood sheets are laid down to form a subfloor and covered with just about any finished flooring you want.

Next, conceal those ugly basement walls with 2' x 4' wall framing. Why? Because framed walls can hold insulation and conceal electrical, phone, and cable wires (otherwise, you'll have to run them out in the open, tacking them along the base of the walls). Cover the wall framing with wood or textile paneling or regular drywall (see page 30).

Now, about that ceiling. Since you can't easily move the ducts, pipes, and wires snaking along the basement ceiling, hide them under a suspended ceiling—it's ideal for basement remodeling. Lightweight panels are supported by a grid of metal tracks hung by wires from the ceiling joists (the beams in the basement ceiling). A suspended ceiling is easy to have installed and won't keep you from getting at all those pipes and wires if you need to. The tracks can even support fluorescent lighting panels—and most basements need a lot of light.

 REMODELING DO'S AND DON'TS

✔ Don't remodel unless your basement is free of moisture. Have the dirt around the foundation sloped away from it and gutter water directed 10' away from the foundation.

✔ Turning basement space into an extra sleeping space is tricky because building codes require strict safety measures for exiting in case of a fire. There must be a door or sizable window leading directly to the outside of the house as an emergency exit. Some building codes also require a certain amount of headroom. Check with your building department before you begin.

✔ Basement posts or columns usually can't be moved, but the beams they support can sometimes be recessed into the framing above to gain much-needed headroom.

✔ Specify metal studs instead of wood ones to ward off any problems with pests.

✔ Don't forget storage space—recreation rooms and playrooms need plenty!

✔ Plan to rebuild—or at least refine—the basement stairway. Stairs leading to a finished living space below need to be better-looking than those heading down to a raw basement.

Fabric-covered fiberboards usually come in 4' x 8' panels in various colors. As wallcoverings they not only add a nice touch of warmth to a basement, but they also help to reduce sound.

FLOATING FLOOR SOURCES

Homasote 800-257-9491

Kahrs Int'l. 415-341-8400

Northstar
Hardwood 888-385-4545

PANELING SOURCES

Kemlite (fiberglass) . 800-435-0080

Homasote (fabric). . 800-257-9491

Sheoga (wood) 440-834-1710

SUSPENDED CEILING SOURCES

Armstrong 800-233-3823

Interfinish 800-560-5758

USG Interiors 800-874-4968

When cabin fever sends you screaming out the door, use that energy to work on improving the outside of the house. Remember, some people still judge a book by its cover.

EXTERIOR

EXTERIOR

Viewed from the outside, a house can reveal how well it functions not only as a shelter but also as a gracious living space. To get smart about its exterior, review the names of the items numbered here, and read on.

EXTERIOR DOORS

1 . . . STORM DOOR

2 . . . SAFETY GLASS

3 . . . KEYED STORM-DOOR HANDLE

4 . . . EXTERIOR DOOR

SIDING/ROOF

5 . . . VINYL SIDING

6 . . . ASPHALT SHINGLES

7 . . . CHIMNEY

8 . . . CHIMNEY CAP (for gas chimney or prefab fireplace)

9 . . . GUTTER

10 . . . DOWNSPOUT

11 . . . ELBOW

12 . . . GABLE VENT

WINDOWS

13 . . . DOUBLE-HUNG WINDOW

14 . . . MUNTINS (or mullions)

15 . . . DECORATIVE SHUTTER

PORCH

16 . . . CONCRETE WALKWAY

17 . . . BRICK ENTRY STEPS

18 . . . WOOD POST

19 . . . WROUGHT-IRON RAILING

20 . . . CEMENT FLOOR

21 . . . PORCH LIGHT (not seen)

22 . . . DECORATIVE TRIM

GARAGE

23 . . . SINGLE ROLL-UP DOOR

24 . . . GARAGE-DOOR HANDLE

25 . . . GARAGE-DOOR LOCK

26 . . . ASPHALT DRIVEWAY

27 . . . GARAGE-DOOR LIGHT

28 . . . KEY PAD FOR ELECTRIC GARAGE-DOOR OPENER

UTILITIES

29 . . . METER

HOME SECURITY

30 . . . MOTION-SENSOR LIGHT

EXTERIOR DOORS

First rule: An exterior door must not leak or let in drafts—to say nothing of unwanted visitors. If there are drafts, seal them off with weather stripping (either foam or beaded metal strips) that are glued or nailed around the doorjamb.

Second rule: For safety's sake and for ease of access, always light the area around exterior doors. In particular, you need light sources near the door. A door with glass panels and sidelights can add to the light inside and out, but be careful that the panels don't compromise your locks (see page 163).

Third rule: The material a door is made from must weather the elements well. Most exterior doors are one of two types: solid wood or an insulating foam core covered with steel or fiberglass. Solid wood is the traditional favorite. Foam-core doors, which are better insulated than wood and require less maintenance, are particularly suited to cold climates. Steel-covered doors are superstrong and offer top security, but they need painting periodically to prevent rusting. Fiberglass-covered doors are lightweight and virtually maintenance-free; they look like wood yet take stain well, and they don't swell the way wood doors do—naturally, they are the most expensive doors on the market.

Exterior doors should be protected by an overhang or porch to shield both the entryway and those who are entering from rough weather.

A door with glass panels combined with a sidelight lets daylight into the entrance hallway and interior light out onto the porch.

Glass doors maximize light. Building codes specify that break-resistant tempered glass be used.

You can extend the life of an exterior door by adding an aluminum or vinyl storm door. It also will reduce heat loss. Some storm doors come with removable glass and screen panels, for making quick switches as the seasons change.

TIME FACTOR

REPLACE	CARPENTER'S TIME
Exterior door	2–3 hrs
Exterior lock	½ hr

 TROUBLE • Drafts under a door? Get a sturdy door sweep (a strip of rubber that attaches to the bottom edge of the door) to help block cold air. For wood doors, which expand and contract, you may want to invest in an adjustable threshold; you can raise or lower its height simply by turning several screws.

• Screen door slams? Get a pneumatic door closer, which slows the door's action and prevents it from banging shut.

DOOR SOURCES

Caradon Doors
(Peachtree) 888-888-3814

Morgan Mfg. 800-766-1992

Pease Industries 800-883-6677

Simpson Door Co. . 800-952-4057

Stanley Door
Systems 800-521-2752

Therma-Tru Corp. . 800-537-8827

Weather Shield 800-477-6808

SIDING

The only real maintenance required for vinyl siding such as the type shown here is hosing it down occasionally when it gets dirty. To reach the upper levels of the house, rent a pressure washer.

Well-maintained siding adds clout to a home's curb appeal, while dilapidated siding sends the message that nobody cares. When choosing siding material—whether for new construction or a face-lift—don't forget to evaluate maintenance requirements as well as looks and cost.

Don't buy a material, no matter how lovely, if you don't think you'll be able to keep up with upkeep. Stress-free siding means one thing: low maintenance. Wood-grain-finish vinyl fits that bill—it needs no painting because the color permeates the material. Vinyl also wears better than aluminum siding, which is seldom used on houses anymore.

Another popular choice, owing to its classic look, is wood. A major disadvantage is the maintenance it requires—painting, staining, or sealing every three to seven years. If primed first, it will hold paint longer. Redwood or cedar shingles and shakes need less care than painted wood does, but they cost more.

Brick lasts many years and needs little maintenance, but it is expensive. Stucco is traditional for warm climates, but it is complicated to apply and requires occasional repairs for cracks.

Brick comes in shades of beige, yellow, red, and brown. Weathered antique brick that is salvaged from old buildings and painted brick that has been allowed to weather are especially prized.

Wooden clapboard can be painted or stained any color. Decorator advice: light colors make a house appear closer to the curb; dark colors make it look as if it's set back.

Cedar shakes and shingles take on a soft gray color after a year or two, while shingles made of redwood retain some of their russet hue even after they have weathered.

 TROUBLE • White mineral deposits on brick? It's called efflorescence. If it really bothers you, simply scrub it off with a stiff brush and a weak solution of muriatic acid (available at your local hardware store). But pay attention if it returns—it can be a sign that moisture is entering the wall, either through cracks or faulty flashing, and repair is needed.

• Crumbling joints in old brick siding? Brick is typically much more durable than the mortar joints holding the wall together. Fix cracked or crumbling joints as soon as possible. Called repointing, the process involves chiseling out about an inch of damaged mortar, removing the debris with a spray of water, and filling the joint with fresh mortar.

• Damaged shakes or shingles? Here's how they are replaced. First, each broken shingle is split with a chisel and pulled out. Exposed nails are pried out, and any concealed nails are cut off with a mini-hacksaw. New shingles are trimmed to fit, then slid in place and nailed down.

 SHORTCUTS • If you live in a wood-sided house and want to get vinyl siding, install the new siding over the old (provided that it's in decent condition). It saves rip-out time and the cost of hauling away the old siding, and gives you added insulation. However, a layer of rigid insulation board should be installed between the wood and the vinyl.

• Termites feed on wood. Keep a minimum distance of 8" between the ground and any wood siding.

SIDING MATH

Vinyl siding is half as expensive as wood shingles or shakes because vinyl costs less and is installed faster. Moreover, vinyl siding is less expensive to maintain. Brick and brickface are the most costly of all, because of the additional labor and time required to install them.

SIDING RESOURCES

BRICK/BRICKFACE

Boren Clay
Products 800-277-5000

Brick Institute of
America 703-620-0010

VINYL

Alcoa 800-621-7466

Mastic Products . . . 800-627-8426

Owens Corning . . . 800-438-7465

Wolverine 800-823-1488

WOOD

Cedar Shake and
Shingle Bureau 206-453-1323

Georgia Pacific 800-284-5347

Western Wood Products
Association 503-224-3930

WINDOWS

Wooden shutters like these are hung on hinges and held open with shutter dogs, such as the curly ones shown here. Plastic shutters are nailed to the house's siding and cannot be closed.

The windows are the eyes of the house, so make them pretty. But beware, good looks can mask energy waste. Inefficient windows can account for as much as 20 percent of heat and air-conditioning loss.

Windows should be tightly sealed so water doesn't get in, and heated air doesn't get out during winter. Older windows in houses built where winter weather is severe usually come with storm windows. These detachable glass panes fit over the regular windows to insulate against the cold. In hurricane country, windows can be fitted with metal panels that fasten over them when storms threaten.

New super-duper energy-efficient glass windows don't need storms. Most newer windows are double-glazed—two panes of glass with a vacuum between them for insulation. To get even more insulating power, look for triple-glazed windows—three panes. Or buy panes made of Low-E glass—it has a special coating that cuts down on heat transfer and rays that fade fabric furnishings.

If you need to replace a window, there are two ways to go: one with no frame, called sash-replacement, or one with a frame, called prehung (see pages 82–83). Both are available in wood, vinyl, or vinyl-clad wood (the vinyl versions need no painting or caulking). If an old window frame is sound, a sash-replacement window is all that's needed. But if an old window frame is split or rotting, replace both frame and window with a new, prehung window; its frame includes both jamb and side channels.

TIME FACTOR	
REPLACE	CONTRACTOR'S TIME
Window sash with jamb	2 hrs
Prehung window	3 hrs

EASY INSULATING

CHECKLIST ✔Find out whether you have air leaks. Light a candle and move it around the frame of every window. (Use caution—don't set your drapes or furnishings on fire.) Wherever the flame flickers, you've got air leaks that should be sealed.

✔Put weather stripping on the top and bottom sash of each window (see page 82).

✔Apply caulk along the edges of each window frame where it meets the interior wall. Do the same on the outside where the window trim meets the siding.

✔If you live in a climate that's extremely hot or cold, consider installing interior insulating shutters, or at least insulating curtains. Either can lessen the effects of cold drafts or intense sunlight; they will not only help to moderate your heating and cooling expenses, but will also make your house far more comfortable in the bargain.

✔If fog or moisture buildup develops between the panes of insulated windows, the seal has been broken. Have them replaced.

This hopper window, installed in a basement, opens near the ceiling to allow warm, moist air to escape before it damages the insulation.

Window awnings made of fabric must be removed in winter unless the climate in your area is very mild.

TROUBLE • Rattling screens? On old windows, screens may become loose because the window has warped. Try tacking weather stripping around the edges of the screen for a snugger fit.

• Strong sun? Install awnings—made of aluminum, fiberglass, or retractable canvas—over the windows to protect the interior of the house from heat and keep furnishings and draperies from fading.

• Allergies? Here's an ironic twist. Insulated windows are so tightly sealed that fresh air can't get into the house. That's not so good if you are allergic to things *inside* (house dust, pet hair, etc.). But don't open the windows; instead, have your heating contractor install special ventilation or filtering systems.

WINDOW MANUFACTURERS

Andersen Windows 800-426-4261

Hurd Millwork Co. . 800-433-4873

Marvin Windows . . 800-346-5128

Pella Corp 800-847-3552

WINDOW ACCESSORIES SOURCES

Eide Industries 800-422-6827

Renovators Supply, Inc. (catalog) 800-659-2211

Shutters, Inc. 800-548-3336

Vixen Hill 800-423-2766

TRADE ASSOCIATION

National Wood Window and Door Assoc. 800-223-2301

PORCHES

Porch steps are governed by rigorous building codes, which require, among other things, that the steps be at least as wide as the front door. Steps that are even wider help to give the entry a generous, welcoming look.

Nothing says relax like a porch. But porches are usually constructed of wood, and because they are so close to Mother Nature, the wood needs regular maintenance. Wood flooring should be coated annually with preservative and deck enamel. (In case you wonder, as you paint, that slope in the floor is there to allow water to roll off.) Railings also need regular painting. If railings are wrought iron, use paint made specifically for exterior metal surfaces. So much for relaxing.

Deteriorating steps, railings, and walkways can be problematic to replace. For repairs on existing structures, you probably won't need a permit, but building a new entryway or enlarging steps or walkways will likely be governed by strict building codes and may require a permit. Local regulations might even dictate which paving materials to use for a sidewalk. Be prudent; check with your local building department before beginning such a project.

Don't forget electrical work. The minimum lighting requirement is a bulb located near the entrance (but not too near, or else the bugs it attracts will fly into the house). And in a warm climate, the breezes wafted by a ceiling fan can make a big porch most inviting.

 ## ENCLOSING A PORCH

CHECKLIST

✔ Unless you're very handy, call a professional to enclose your porch; the job requires advanced building skills. In many areas local building laws also must be adhered to, since the enclosed porch may be regarded as a new room.

✔ A porch can be enclosed with either removable panels or permanent panels attached to the posts. Removable panels of screen or glass, in wood or metal frames, must be stored when not in use. Permanent panels may destroy any feeling of openness, but they do offer more privacy and protection from weather.

✔ An inexpensive option: Enclose a porch with trellis panels (sold in most home centers and lumberyards in 4' x 6' panels). Just nail them to the posts and plant vines or climbing roses to grow on them.

SHORTCUTS

• Anchor wooden porch posts in concrete footings to protect them from termites, water damage, and rot.

• Save time when painting porch railings (wood or wrought iron) by using a painting mitt—a thick cloth mitten worn on your hand. Dip it into the paint, then rub the paint on. It's quicker than using a brush.

• If you have no room for a front porch, consider putting up a portico above the entrance to your house to protect the front door (and visitors) from the elements.

In cold climates, extend the time you can use your porch each year by installing removable windowed panels.

WALKWAY PAVING MATERIALS

Pros and Cons of materials you can choose for walkways:

CONCRETE—Pro: Cheap, quick to install, durable, easy to repair. Con: Sterile-looking, discolors over time.

PRE-CAST PAVING STONES (made of concrete, usually with a pigment or texture added)—Pro: quick to install, durable, moderately priced, pretty. Con: Must be installed on base that is absolutely level, or else stones tend to crack.

BRICKS—Pro: Beautiful, fairly durable. Con: Expensive, prone to cracking, need maintenance.

FLAGSTONE—Pro: Beautiful, durable. Con: Expensive.

PORCH PRODUCT SOURCES

Americana Building
Products/Hindman. . 800-851-0865

Craft-Bilt. 800-422-8577

Four Seasons
Sunrooms. 800-368-7732

Harvey Industries. . . 800-225-5724

National
Manufacturing, Inc. . 800-444-9978

U.S. Sky. 800-323-5017

DECKS

Most safety codes call for railings on decks. If children will be using a deck, a railing can be an important safety feature, even if the local code does not require one.

A deck works like an outdoor room, providing an open space free of mud and dust for cooking, dining, and partying. Building a deck is one of those home improvements that will usually almost pay for itself upon resale of your home.

Planning is key. A deck's location is as important as its looks. You may want easy access from the kitchen, living room, or family room. Perhaps you'll need a bit of privacy from the neighbors. Also, check the amount of sun the area gets; otherwise, you might have to splurge on an awning.

Now think about the deck itself. Is it to be a simple platform, or must it be raised to accommodate a sloping lot? To test your final design, tape off the approximate deck area on the lawn, then fill the space with furniture, grill, playhouse, and whatever else will live on the deck. That done, consider what's to be built-in. Do you want built-in benches? A built-in grill? A platform for a hot tub? Be sure to allow for lights and electrical outlets in your design.

Don't forget to obtain a building permit. Your local building code lists specifications for such things as supports, railings, and steps. The code is there for your own protection and will help guarantee a good job. It also outlines setback requirements, which define how far away from your property's perimeter any structure must be.

DECK MATERIALS

CHECKLIST ✔ Redwood, cedar, and mahogany are beautiful, durable, and resistant to decay, but they can be expensive. (Make sure the contractor doesn't use galvanized nails on cedar; they'll cause dark spots.)

✔ Pressure-treated (PT) wood is fairly inexpensive and durable, and it weathers to a silvery gray. It has been soaked in arsenic, which preserves it but can cause it to dry out faster. Applying a coat of sealer will slow down the drying process.

✔ Wood-plastic hybrids, called composite decking, and solid-plastic PVC decking don't splinter, split, or rot and need no periodic finishing. However, they are expensive, and color may vary from piece to piece. Discuss how to handle the color problem with your contractor before signing a contract.

TROUBLE • Is your back in a knot from the annual applications of the sealer that preserves your wood decks? Spare yourself by renting or buying a sprayer to apply it.

• To cut down even more on sealing time, go for the best-quality finishing product you can afford. You'll spend more money but work less, since one coat of a high-quality product usually produces the same finish you'd get from two coats of a lesser-quality product.

• Deck looking grungy? Spruce it up with a deck cleaner/brightener, which comes in bleach and nonbleach formulas. (The bleach type will lighten the deck's color somewhat.)

Add visual interest to a deck with different levels connected by wide steps (top right). A pergola (right) made of lattice work or a semi-opaque plastic will shade a sun-drenched deck.

TIME FACTOR	
INSTALL	**CONTRACTOR'S TIME**
New deck (without drying time for concrete)	**3 days**
Apply seal	**1 hr**
NOTE: Deck size 12' × 12' × 3'	

DECK RESOURCES

Brock Deck	800-365-3625
DEC-K-ING	800-804-6288
DecTec.	800-268-1078
Duradek.	800-338-3568
Gerber Ind.	800-844-1401
Heritage Vinyl.	800-473-3623

GARAGES

The cutlines in the concrete driveway allow it to expand and contract during the seasons without cracking. Ideally, the garage doors should match the architectural style of your house.

They don't have to be boring. Garage doors are available in many styles, and can actually lend some character to an otherwise featureless space. They come in single or double sizes, with the double doors providing the easiest access. The most popular look is real wood. It's inexpensive, but if you want it to stand up to the weather, you have to repaint it often. Other materials that require less maintenance are aluminum, steel, and fiberglass; many doors made of these materials are designed to resemble wooden ones. The doors come in two types—roll-ups (composed of four or more hinged sections) or single-piece tilt-ups. The roll-up advantage: they need zero clearance in front of the door to open.

For the ultimate in convenience, install an automatic garage-door opener —you won't know how you ever did without one. To avoid deadly accidents, newer models have a built-in auto-reversing mechanism, which can be activated by physical contact with the door or by breaking an infrared beam. The contact device stops and reverses the door within two seconds after it hits any object during descent. The noncontact mechanism, which is thought by many to offer the best protection, works by directing an infrared beam across the garage entrance near the ground; when the beam is interrupted by any object, the closing door is automatically reversed.

DRIVEWAYS

Of all driveway surfaces, *gravel* is the most economical to install. It's hard to clear leaves and debris off gravel, but that's also part of its rural charm. Its surface, however, can rut and become muddy after a time, and as you clear snow from it, you may remove some of the gravel. *Asphalt* (or "black-top") is more costly than gravel, but it can be raked and shoveled easily. The surface can be slick; mix sand with the sealer to give it "bite." The asphalt does have to be resealed every three to four years, or else it tends to crack and deteriorate. *Concrete*, the most durable of the three, requires the least amount of maintenance, but it is the most expensive. Alas, it does absorb oil stains and can develop cracks. Cutlines in the surface help it expand and contract without cracking; if small cracks appear, fill them in to prevent them from deteriorating. Have a masonry sealer applied every year, especially in cold climates, to fend off corrosion caused by road salt.

Nothing says country like a gravel driveway. Gravel comes in various colors to accent your house: dark gray, green, blue or red.

SHORTCUTS

• Blot up an unsightly oil spill on a garage floor by covering it with a layer of sawdust or cat litter. Let it sit overnight, then sweep it up.

• Organize the garage into storage centers—as in a kitchen—by placing tools and materials for gardening, auto repair, sports, and other activities in separate areas. Take advantage of wall and ceiling space. Lightweight bikes can hibernate on screw hooks attached to wall studs or ceiling joists. Sports balls and other lightweight stuff can be stowed in an old hammock hung across a car bay. If your garage has a gabled roof, place a sheet or two of plywood across the ceilings joists and store bulky seasonal objects up there.

GARAGE DOOR RESOURCES

Amarr Garage
Doors. 910-744-5100

General American
Door Co. 800-323-0813

Genie Co. 800-654-3643

Overhead Door . . . 800-929-3667

Stanley Door
Systems 800-521-2752

TIME FACTOR

INSTALL	GARAGE-DOOR CONTRACTOR'S TIME
Tilt-up door	1 hr
Roll-up door	1 hr

HOME SECURITY

Outdoor lighting enhances an entryway and, at the same time, creates a bright pathway to the door that can discourage intruders.

 CHECKLIST IDEAS TO KEEP YOUR HOME SECURE

✔ Keep the doors and windows locked at all times to deter intruders and to fulfill your insurance policy requirements.

✔ Trim plantings located close to the house. Overgrown boughs can hide intruders.

✔ Sliding patio doors are usually easy to jimmy. Think about investing in either a bar lock or a keyed dead bolt at the base of the door. Failing that, put a dowel or an old broomstick in the door track to block the door if someone attempts to slide it open.

✔ Invest in good lighting and make sure all sides of the house and yard are well lit. Floodlights that are equipped with a motion sensor will shine bright beams on anybody approaching your house. Place them high enough so that a burglar won't be able to unscrew the bulbs.

✔ Put a few interior lights on a timer. The lights can give the impression that you're home, even when you're not.

✔ Install a set of low-voltage lighting. Put lights into pre-dug holes about 8" deep—you hook the cable to the fixtures before embedding the stakes, then cover the cable with mulch. The set comes with a transformer that plugs into a regular household outlet. Its job is to step down the current from 120 volts to 12, which is safer for outdoor lighting and more economical. Consider this option: a photoelectric eye, which automatically switches on the lights at dusk.

✔ Store important papers in a fire-resistant box or file. The files come in models containing one to four drawers. Reinforced fire-resistant safes are even tougher—they can withstand the collapse of a house and are equipped with a heavy-duty lock to deter burglars. Safes can be mounted in a wall or bolted to the floor.

✔ Install a peephole in the front door. Don't rely on a door chain; they can be broken with a good shove on the door.

✔ Change the garage-door opener codes regularly. Never use the one that came with the unit, as it is known to anyone familiar with your door model.

✔ Get a dog. You don't need a fanged monster—an ordinary dog will usually sound the alert if there is a burglar (or a fire).

✔ Don't leave ladders, hammers, or other useful tools outside the house—thieves can use them to break in.

✔ Electronic security systems are expensive but effective. You can install either a wireless or a wired system. Wireless systems consist of individual sensors that respond to body weight, heat, or sounds, each with its own alarm, placed wherever they are needed, and turned off and on by a remote-control touch pad. Wired-systems sensors are connected together and operated by means of a central control panel.

EXTERIOR LOCKS

Not locking the door accounts for half of all burglaries. (More bad news: if there's no forced entry, some insurance companies won't cover your losses!) So get good locks and use them. A cylinder lock with a key-in-knob is fairly easy to pick. It's best to add a *dead-bolt lock* or a *rim lock* to all outside doors. A dead bolt consists of a lock with a horizontal bolt that slides into a metal housing (called a strike plate) in the doorjamb. It locks with a key from the outside and a thumb turn on the inside. The longer the bolt and the sturdier the strike plate, the better. The toughest lock? The rim lock. It fits on the surface of the door, and its horizontal bolt slides into a strike plate mounted on the doorjamb. Like a dead bolt, it can be opened with a key from the outside and a thumb turn inside, or with a key on both sides (best for doors near glass). Smart tip: Use 3"-long screws to securely fasten a rim lock and strike plate to the door and doorjamb.

Dead bolt locks add security to exterior doors.

The thumb turn on this heavy-duty rim lock operates the dead bolt.

✔ Sensors should be positioned in all first-floor doors and windows, but easily accessible second-story windows should be protected, too. For convenience, locate the remote-control touch pad or the control panel near a commonly-used entryway.

✔ You can choose silent alarms, external alarms, or a combination of both. Have your silent alarm rigged to automatically contact a security company or the local police station.

✔ If you have pets that roam the house at night and you want to install an electronic security system, have any body-weight sensors that are installed at door thresholds set for a few pounds more than your pets' maximum weight.

SECURITY RESOURCES

ALARM SYSTEMS

Ademco 800-573-0154

Intellinet 800-899-1372

Napco Security 800-645-9445

LIGHTING

Regent Lighting 800-334-6871

Tiffany Landscape Lighting. 800-882-8112

Toro Co. 800-348-2424

LOCKS

Masterlock Co. 414-444-2800

Schlage Lock Co. . . 415-467-1100

Weiser Lock. 800-677-5625

INDEX

INDEX

RESOURCES

CREDITS

PICTURE

P.7 D. Petku/H. Armstrong Roberts; p. 9 D. Petku/H. Armstrong Roberts; p.10 C. Bucks/H. Armstrong Roberts; p.11 left Alan Magayne-Roshak/Third Coast Stock Source, right Jane Grushow/Grant Heilman; p.12 Susan Oristaslio/Esto; p.13 top C. Johnson/Camerique/H. Armstrong Roberts; center and bottom Ron Passaro, Res-I-Tec, Inc.; p.14 both H. Abernathy/H. Armstrong Roberts; p.15 R. Krubner/H. Armstrong Roberts; p.16 C. Bucks/H. Armstrong Roberts; p.17 John Nienhuis/Third Coast Stock Source; p.18 C. Johnson/Camerique/H. Armstrong Roberts; p.19 David Frazier/The Stock Market; p.20 Patti McConville/ The Image Bank; p.21 Brian Vanden Brink; p.23 Paris Ceramics; p.24-25 Hickory White Co.; p.26 Premier™ Wood Floors; p.27 top left Laufen Ceramic Tile, top right Armstrong World Industries, bottom Historic Floors of Oshkosh Inc.; p.28 Hickory White Co.; p.29 left Basset Furniture Industries. Inc., right Scott Frances/Esto; p.31 all left ©The Reader's Digest Association, Inc. / Photo by Michael Molkenthin, right Drexel Heritage Furnishings; p.33 Drexel Heritage Furnishings; p.34 Broyhill Furniture Industries, Inc.; p.35 top and center left ©The Reader's Digest Association, Inc. / Photo by Michael Molkenthin, top right Merillat Industries, Inc., center left Skills and Tools, center right Merillat Industries, Inc., Bottom left KraftMaid Cabinetry, Inc., bottom right ©The Reader's Digest Association, Inc. / Photo by Michael Molkenthin; p.36 Gramercy; p.37 Pergo; p.39 Heritage Custom Kitchen, Inc.; p.40-41 Whirlpool Home Appliances; p.44 IXL Cabinets; p.45 Heritage Custom Kitchens, Inc.; p.46 top left to right all Merillat Industries, Inc. except second from right KraftMaid Cabinetry, Inc., bottom Merillat Industries, Inc.; p.47 left Amerock Corp.,top right IXL Cabinets, bottom right KraftMaid Cabinetry, Inc.; p.48 Plain & Fancy Custom Cabinetry; p.49 Wilsonart International; p.50 Wilsonart International; p.51 Wilsonart International; p.53 left American Standard, Inc., right Kohler Co.; p.55 both GE Appliances; p.56 Heritage Custom Kitchens, Inc.; p.57 Glidden; p.58 Jenn-Air; p.59 Amana; p.60 GE Appliances; p.61 left GE Appliances, right Jenn-Air; p.62 Tarkett, Inc.; p.63 left Heritage Custom Kitchens, Inc., right Mark Darley/Esto; p.65 Gary Russ/The Image Bank; p.66-67 Randy O'Rourke/The Stock Market; p.68 Heatilator, Inc.; p.69 left Rais & Wittus, Inc., right Taos Furniture®, Santa Fe, NM; p.70 Gary Russ/The Image Bank; p.71 Pergo; p.72 Andersen Windows, Inc.; p.75 top Lisl Dennis/The Image Bank, bottom Gary Russ/ The Image Bank; p.74 top Steven B. Mays, center and bottom First Alert, Inc.; p.75 top Steven B. Mays, bottom Leslie-Locke, Inc.; p.77 Andersen Windows, Inc.; p.78-79 Lexington Furniture Industries; p.80 left and right Simpson Door Co.; p.81 top Caradco Windows & Patio Doors, bottom ©The Reader's Digest Association, Inc. / Photo by Michael Molkenthin; p.83 left Weather Shield Windows and Doors, right Marvin Windows & Doors; p.84 York Wallcoverings; p.85 all ©The Reader's Digest Association, Inc. / Photo by Michael Molkenthin; p.86 Glidden; p.87 all Wools of New Zealand except bottom left Daltonian Carpet and Cushion, Inc.; p.88 The Closet Factory; p.89 Poliform USA, Inc.; p.90 Lexington Furniture Industries; p.91 Broyhill Furniture Industries, Inc; p.93 Techline Furniture; p.95 Waterworks; p.98 Tile Promotion Board; p.99 Kohler; p.101 left Kohler Co, center St. Thomas Creations, right American Standard, Inc.; p.103 top St.Thomas Creations, center left Peerless Faucet Co, center right American Standard, Inc., bottom Grohe; p.105 left & right American Standard, Inc., center Kohler Co.; p.106 AmericanShower and Bath, Corp.; p.107 left Aquaglass, Corp., top Waterworks, bottom right Kohler Co.; p.108 Interbath, Inc.; p.109 top left Waterworks, top right and middle left Kohler Co., middle right St.Thomas Creations, bottom Franklin Brass MFG, Co.; p.110 both Kohler Co.; p.111 left Kohler Co., right American Shower & Bath ; p.113 top left Waterworkds, bottom left St Thomas Creations, top right Brian Vanden Brink; p.114 top Paris Ceramics, bottom Tile Promotion Board; p.115 left and middle Country Floors, right Laufen Ceramic Tile; p.116 St. Thomas Creations; p.117 all Tarkett, Inc.; p.119 Steven B. Mays; p.122 Owens Corning; p.123 left CertainTeed, Corp. right Steven B. Mays; p.124 Brian Vanden Brink; p.125 top and center Owens Corning, bottom M.C.A. Clay Roof Tile; p.126 Celotex Corp.; p.127 left Owens Corning, right American Metal Products; p.128 The Celotex Corp.; p.129 both Brian Vanden Brink; p.131 Steven B. Mays; p.135 top Zoeller Pump Co., center and bottom ©The Reader's Digest Association, Inc. / Photo by Michael Molkenthin; p.136 both Steven B. Mays; p.137 Carrier's Residential Products Group; p.138 thru 140 Steven B. Mays; p.141 from Every Day Home Repairs, ©Cowles Creative Publishing; p.143 Maytag Appliances; p.144 Juno Lighting. Inc.; p.145 Homasote Co.; p.147 Tom Knibbs/The Image Bank; p.148-149 Steven B. Mays; p.150 Simpson Door Co.; p.151 left Weather Shield Windows and Doors, right E. Cooper/H. Armstrong Roberts; p.152 Owens Corning; p.153 left Boren Brick, center Glidden, right Brian Vanden Brink; p.154 Vixen Hill Manufacturing Co.; p.155 left Steven B. Mays, right Eide Industries, Inc.; p.156-157 Steven B. Mays; p.158 Four Seasons Sunrooms; p.159 both California Redwood Association; p.160 H. Gariety/H. Armstrong Roberts; p.161 M. Gibson/H. Armstrong Roberts; p.162 The Toro Co.; p.163 top ©The Reader's Digest Association, Inc. / Photo by Michael Molkenthin, bottom Alpan, Inc.

ILLUSTRATION

John Hovell:
Cover art, pages 42, 43, 98, 99, 120, 121, 132 ,133

Robert Steimle:
pages 30, 52, 54, 82, 92, 100, 102, 104, 108, 134, 142